Second Lieutenant R.C. Sherriff, possibly in 1916, reproduced by permission
of Kingston Grammar School and The Surrey History Centre

Robert Gore-Langton

JOURNEY'S END

THE CLASSIC WAR PLAY EXPLORED

OBERON BOOKS
LONDON

WWW.OBERONBOOKS.COM

First published in 2013 by Oberon Books Ltd
521 Caledonian Road, London N7 9RH
Tel: +44 (0) 20 7607 3637 / Fax: +44 (0) 20 7607 3629
e-mail: info@oberonbooks.com
www.oberonbooks.com

A catalogue record for this book is available from the British Library.

PB ISBN: 978-1-84943-395-2
E ISBN: 978-1-84943-872-8

Printed, bound and converted
by CPI Group (UK) Ltd, Croydon, CR0 4YY.

Visit www.oberonbooks.com to read more about all our books and to
buy them. You will also find features, author interviews and news of any
author events, and you can sign up for e-newsletters so that you're always
first to hear about our new releases.

For Grenville and Elizabeth

Contents

Acknowledgements

My biggest thank you is to my wife Sue, for putting up with the trenches and me. I am indebted also to the director David Grindley who couldn't have been more enthusiastic or helpful.

Sherriff was a generous benefactor of the Boy Scouts and his old school. I am grateful to the Scouts Association, to Kingston Grammar School and to Curtis Brown Group Ltd. London for their permission to quote from Sherriff's unpublished letters, papers and diary, his essay 'The English Public Schools in The Great War' in *Promise of Greatness* (1968) edited by G. A. Panichas, *No Leading Lady* (1968) and the novel *Journey's End* (1930). The Society of Authors kindly gave permission on behalf of the Bernard Shaw estate to quote Shaw's letter to RCS. The quotations from *Journey's End* come from the Penguin Classics playscript by permission of Penguin Books. Despite my best efforts, if I have not managed to trace any copyright holders I apologise for any unintended breach.

I owe thanks to Geoffrey Streatfeild, David Haig and other cast members of *Journey's End* who contributed (without fee) their thoughts and time to either the book, the radio project or both. I am grateful for the support of Nicola Beauman, publisher of Sherriff's novels and founder of Persephone Books. I also thank Major Richard Streatfeild for use of his blog post, Simon Hollis, Gen. Sir Michael Rose, Dr Michael and Annie Dixon, Max Arthur, Andrew Rissik, Angela Stockbridge, Julie Macpherson and David Twining-Harris. I also thank my fellow theatre critics who I have quoted.

Introduction

At the time of writing, *War Horse* is still a huge hit. But *Journey's End* is unique in being the only Great War play by a veteran to have any longevity and the only one to be set entirely in a trench. This book comes out of an encounter with the play back in 2004. It hit me like a World War One whizzbang. What was so surprising was that despite being the most successful war play since *Henry V* nobody seemed to know anything about its author.

Annoyingly, Sherriff's autobiography leaves out his entire war experience. But I discovered what I could, made several trips to the Front (bumping into windswept parties of British schoolchildren doing *Journey's End* at GCSE) and a programme for Radio 4. David Grindley and his cast came into talk about the play.

Anyway, it left room for a longer story about the background to the play. That is what this book is – an account of the front line context, the staging and the afterlife of a classic war play. It ends with a detailed look at the most recent West End production, the best since the first. I have not attempted a biography of Sherriff but the basic facts of his life are these: Robert Cedric Sherriff (1896-1975) was an insurance clerk from Hampton Wick (on the Thames) who joined up. He was commissioned into the 9/East Surrey Regiment as a second lieutenant and his active service in France was from the end of September 1916 to the beginning of August 1917 when he was wounded in the face at Passchendaele. He recovered in England and never returned to the front. Sherriff was demobbed in 1919 with the rank of captain and went back to his old firm as a loss adjuster in the Thames Valley.

He wrote several amateur dramas as fundraisers for his local rowing club in the mid-1920s. His final play was not for the oarsmen but for himself. 'All the previous plays had been about imaginary people in imaginary situations, and now for the first time I was writing about something real, about men I had lived with and knew so well that every line they spoke came from them and not from me.'[1]

On paper it had nothing going for it – no leading lady, no French windows or anyone for tennis. Worse, it was about the war and war plays were then considered a deadly snore by theatre managements. It was put on by the not for profit Stage Society in late 1928 with the young Laurence Olivier, before transferring to the Savoy Theatre early the following year with Colin Clive replacing him in the lead.

The show was wildly praised, became a huge box office smash in London. It was soon playing in twenty-six languages in most of the capitals in Europe; it was a hit in America, Australia and the far reaches of the Empire. It clocked up a record-breaking run of 593 performances in the West End and ended up as both a film and a novel. The published play sold 175,000 copies. It made Sherriff and his producer rich men. It also launched the career of the cult film director James Whale.

Rejecting the theatre, Sherriff decided to become a mature student with a view to schoolmastering. He went up to Oxford but abandoned his History degree for a Hollywood contract to write the screenplay for *The Invisible Man*. He became a highly successful jobbing screenwriter and a bestselling novelist. His fiction masterpiece was *The Fortnight in September* (1931) and his films in the late Thirties and Forties included *Goodbye Mr Chips*, *The Four Feathers*, *Lady Hamilton*, *Mrs. Miniver* and *Odd Man Out* among others. His screenwriting career ended with *The Dam Busters* in 1955. He died in 1975 at the age of seventy-nine, by then totally forgotten.

Today his name rests on his war play. They say a lot of war poetry is love poetry in disguise. Certainly *Journey's End* is rooted in love. The one big affair of Sherriff's life was with C Company of the 9/East Surrey. His play reflects his extraordinary

1   R.C. Sherriff, *No Leading Lady*, p.37

compassion for the men he served alongside. His play doesn't ask what the war meant: 'Will you take apricots, sir' is about its most probing question. But it reflects the intense brazier glow of the comradeship he never forgot.

Sherriff's entry in biographical dictionaries states that he won the Military Cross. He didn't. In fact he was not naturally very courageous. His ten and half months in France was plagued by constant fear – fear of shells and a fear of failing to do his job properly. He tried desperately like all the other schoolboys in uniform to be brave. He underwent some sort of crisis in the spring of 1917.

His problem was there was no such thing as 'all quiet' on the Western Front. No one was ever psychologically off-guard. Everyone was strung out and exhausted. Sherriff hated the tension and saw it in others; he was acutely aware of the give-away yawns of nervousness before a raid, a trembling hand lighting up a smoke after a near-miss shell. When Harold Pinter saw *Journey's End* in 2004 he sent the actor Geoffrey Streatfeild (playing the nerve-shattered Captain Stanhope) and the cast a generous letter of congratulations. Pinter knew a good play and a pregnant pause when he heard one.

Like a lot of huge hits, *Journey's End* turned out to be uninfluential. It did, however, inspire Noël Coward to write a peacetime sequel but that was unproduced. A generation later, in the Sixties, the play was the object of pathological hatred from Joan Littlewood and it can claim to be a negative inspiration for her famous musical *Oh What A Lovely War*.

What was Sherriff like? He seems to have been gentle, straitlaced, highly sporty, hero-worshipping, deeply conservative and proudly unintellectual. He had terrific empathy for others and a good sense of humour but little self-esteem. He never quite saw what everyone else did in his play. He was very cautious of his own fame and in the end he became reclusive. The young Alec Guinness would have been perfect casting as Sherriff, the benign, slightly inscrutable insurance man in bicycle clips who got lucky.

His love life is a total mystery, not that it's relevant to the play. He never married and lived with his mother nearly all her life. Most people connected to the play today seem to have intuited that he was gay – a likely hunch I'd say. He seems to have diverted all his bachelor energies entirely into his work, his garden and his coin collection. He was proud of his large Esher house and the Rolls-Royce he bought with the play's proceeds. He went from being a £7 a week loss adjuster to a £1000 a week playwright almost overnight and the story of *Journey's End* is one of incredible jackpot success. Today the local arts scene in Surrey is a major benefactor of the play through the R.C. Sherriff Trust.

Most academic literary historians – who are reliably useless on a live medium like theatre – have no time for the play. For them it's naïve, un-ironic and it smacks too much of the rugby pitch and school dorm. Actors and theatre critics on the other hand have always had a natural regard for the play because they inhabit its intended zone of impact – the theatre.

Journey's End for all its tragedy is certainly not the play Robert Graves or Siegfried Sassoon might have written. It came out of a belief that the war had a point and a purpose. Sherriff remained deeply proud of his regiment all his life. In the end his own verdict on his war was a vote for it: 'there had been bad times in France but all in all it had been a magnificent, memorable experience.'[2]

Journey's End is an alternative to the 'gas and ghastliness' narrative of the war poets. The play is tragic because everyone in it dies. But it also depicts the war being fought with greasy tea, Gold Flake and a weapon less available to the enemy – a sense of humour. It's worth remembering that to the vast majority of Britons at the time, the war was a just and necessary fight against what was effectively a German military dictatorship, one that had brutally invaded Belgium and France and threatened the channel ports. The Kaiser had it coming. He may be a war criminal these days but in 1928 Douglas Haig, commander of

2   Ibid., p.317

the British forces, was mourned by vast numbers who lined the streets in the greatest state funeral since Wellington's. The same crowd queued at the box office months later to see *Journey's End*. The Savoy Theatre became a place of pilgrimage for anyone who had lost someone – and that was almost everyone.

There's an extraordinary gulf between Sherriff's view of his own drama and that of its pacifist producer Maurice Browne, who saw it was an ardent peace play. Sherriff wasn't at all sure about that. He was certainly extremely careful not to tarnish in any way the sacrifice made by his friends and countrymen. Theirs was an incredibly tough and unself-centred generation. They didn't think they were dying in vain and nor I believe do the characters in *Journey's End*.

One other thing: it is a play about officers. This is because Sherriff was a commissioned officer himself and he wrote what he knew. Far from being a cushy number, being a junior officer was exceptionally dangerous. When there was fighting to be done their job was to lead from the front, hence their massive and disproportionate loss. At certain points of the war they could expect to survive about six weeks. It is also far from being a drama of doomed young toffs. Sherriff was not a public schoolboy and his play accurately reflects the mixed social reality of the officer class in the frontline as it was in late 1916 when he arrived there. Unlike more recent Great War plays such as *Observe the Sons of Ulster Marching Towards the Somme* or *The Accrington Pals* or *The Big Picnic*, all of which have their roots well north of Watford, *Journey's End* is based on a Kitchener battalion from the south of England. The play's ongoing fascination is – to me anyway – its complete authenticity. It lights up the Western Front like a Boche flare. There is nothing else quite like it.

In tracing Sherriff's life from the front, I have used his letters (he wrote several times a week to his parents) from his archive, held at the Surrey History Centre (SHC) in Woking. Sherriff's diary (there was a condensed serialisation in *The Observer* in 1930) dates from October 1916 and ends that Christmas. All quotations I have used are from his handwritten unpaginated copy (hence my lack of page references) held at Kingston Grammar School.

There is no biography of Sherriff but Rosa Maria Bracco's essay on him in *Merchants of Hope* is very insightful, though she approaches the play from a less enamoured and more literary perspective. Mine is a theatre book with lots of gory war details. While I was writing it, Michael Lucas' deeply researched *The Journey's End Battalion: the 9th East Surrey in the Great War* was published and put a blissful end to my struggle with Sherriff's battalion's movements. His is the definitive military history of the unit and it contains valuable information about Sherriff and his comrades. *The History of the East Surrey Regiment* makes little mention of Sherriff but has exciting highlights of the 9th Battalion in action.

Fully Insured

So what actually happens in *Journey's End*? What did the play look like back in 1928 at the Apollo Theatre? The answer is – like nothing before it. A World War One dugout on stage, a small acting area with steps visible up to a trench, a rough timber table, wooden slatted walls, a candle in a bottle and a fug of cigarette smoke, much of it drifting in from the stalls.

We are near St Quentin, twenty-four miles west of Amiens and ninety miles north of Paris, two and a half days before the great German offensive of 21 March 1918. A keen eighteen-year-old ex-public schoolboy, James 'Jimmy' Raleigh, joins C Company, fresh from school – 'they're the kind that do best'. He is the nephew of a general who has arranged for him to join the company of Captain Dennis Stanhope MC, three years older, a prefect whom he worshipped at school for his sporting prowess.

'Uncle' Osborne, a kindly middle-aged, greying ex-schoolmaster and second in command welcomes Raleigh to the trench and warns him that Stanhope has been changed by his years at the front. 'It tells on a man – rather badly.' Stanhope does his job well but he drinks constantly and his nerves are shot to pieces. He resents Raleigh's presence and is cold to him because he holds a candle for Raleigh's sister Madge and does not want reports of his degradation to filter back. 'He'll write to her and tell I reek of whisky all day.'

Stanhope is ordered to arrange a dangerous raid by Headquarters, to snatch a prisoner and gather information about the German attack that they know is imminent. Osborne and Raleigh are chosen as the two officers most likely to succeed on the mission, to go with ten volunteers. Trotter is too fat and Hibbert is not made of the right stuff. Stanhope would go but cannot be spared.

Meanwhile, Hibbert tries to go down the line to see the doctor about his neuralgia. Stanhope thinks he is 'another worm trying to wriggle home' to a comfortable nerve hospital. He pulls his revolver and threatens to shoot him if he leaves. Hibbert waits for the shot that never comes and then breaks down. Stanhope comforts him by praising the way he stood his ground and by confessing to his own fears. Grateful, Hibbert asks him not to mention the incident to the others. Stanhope agrees, as long as Hibbert doesn't 'tell anyone what a blasted funk I am.'

The raid produces one German prisoner and the Colonel is pleased. However, Osborne has been killed along with some other men and Stanhope is deprived of his closest friend and confessor. That evening he, Trotter and Hibbert binge on champagne and chicken in a pre-arranged but now empty celebration of the raid. Raleigh avoids the drunken dinner as it seems to him heartless in view of Osborne's death. Stanhope after years in the trenches is bitterly used to concealing his feelings and brutally accuses the boy, unaccustomed to daily tragedy, of being a prig.

The big attack comes at dawn the next day. Shells rain down. Raleigh is hit immediately and his spine broken. He is carried down to the dugout. Stanhope comforts him, hiding from him the seriousness of the injury and they briefly rekindle their old school friendship. Raleigh dies. Stanhope then goes up top to join the men and repel the big attack. A shell hits the vacant dugout roof, entombing Raleigh's body inside. The play ends with Stanhope and the remaining cast clearly doomed.

That is the outline of the play that would go around the world. Many thought Sherriff wrote the play during the war in which he was killed. But in fact he outlasted The Beatles. So what do we know about him? In old age he was still tall, almost completely bald, not an ounce of fat on him. The last public sighting of him was possibly at the opening of the Thames Ditton branch library in 1971. For a man of his shyness, the event was a nightmare. The District Librarian later wrote about Sherriff's attempted escape in a local newsletter.

He was so panicky at the thought of meeting the audience afterwards that I actually had to stand in the doorway to block his exit so that at least we got half an hour's conversation out of him! He bore me no malice and I several times took sherry with him at his house, Rosebriars. The house contained oak cabinets with a complete collection of Roman coins, his 'portrait gallery of the emperors', as he would call it. Downstairs we would sit and enjoy his excellent sherry, with me sitting normally in an armchair and him sitting sideways on, dangling his long thin legs. He was full of nervous energy, describing to me such episodes as the time his regiment was posted to Glasgow in anticipation of a 'red revolt'.[1]

Sherriff on another occasion gave a local talk about his house, Rosebriars, on Esher Park Avenue (now bulldozed and its large garden developed) and about his interest in archaeology that had led him to dig, with archaeologist Sir Mortimer Wheeler, the Roman villa at Angmering on the Sussex coast, an experience which led to his play about a Roman family in Britain, *The Long Sunset* (1955). He gave a brief description of how *Journey's End* came to be staged in the West End. There are similar short talks he gave in his fluting voice for the BBC in the National Sound Archive. But he left very little trace of himself.

Sherriff grew up in suburban obscurity in a detached house in Hampton Wick, just over the river from Kingston upon Thames, then a tiny village on a tram route. The house (2 Seymour Road) has recently been demolished for redevelopment, Sherriff's name of insufficient note to save it. He was the son of Herbert Hankin Sherriff, an insurance clerk who married Constance Winder, the daughter of an architect from Iver, Buckinghamshire, in 1893. 'Connie' was nineteen when they married.

Herbert and Connie Sherriff produced three children: Beryl was born in 1893, Robert on 6 June 1896, and Cecil (known as 'Bundy') in 1899. Robert's great-grandfather and his ancestors were governors of Aylesbury Gaol, a post that seems to have been hereditary. When the prison passed into military control so ended one hundred

---

1   Esher District Local History Society Newsletter, Winter 2005

years of prison service from the Sherriff family. That meant a dip in the family's social standing in the late Victorian era.

The reason Robert went into insurance is that his father and grandfather were both insurance men. Being 'in the Sun' was secure but very, very dull. Sherriff hated it and so did his father. Herbert Sherriff – a rather Pooterish man who always wanted to be an explorer – spent almost fifty years behind a desk shuffling claim forms. Robert noted that his father started as junior clerk in one corner of the office and forty-five years later ended up in the opposite corner as senior clerk, an average move, he computed, of five inches a year.

For the eccentric Sherriff Snr no amount of fresh air was ever enough. Robert noted in a draft chapter of his father's unpublished autobiography a passion for detail. Nothing was too minute to record. Robert on reading it wrote:

> And so it goes through the years – from Gladstone and Bismarck to Stanley Baldwin and Hitler. On the spare pages at the end of each diary appears a neat summary of his year's achievements. I quote the results of 1912:
> Bicycled 3276 miles.
> Sculled 35 times on river.
> Watched 29 cricket matches.
> Caught 48 mice.
> Stamp collection 2218 – increase in year 143.
> Birds eggs 49.
> 3 colds.
> Late at office 7 times (4 times owing to fog).

In 1929 Sherriff's father wrote in his unputdownable diary:

> Since 1876 I have bicycled 152,729 miles – equally 19 times round the world and over half way to the moon. Had enough of it. Sold bicycle this evening to Brooks in High Street for 35/– and gave bicycle clips to the boy next door.[2]

Of Robert's mother I have found out very little except that he wrote his most revealing letters from the Western Front to her. In middle-age she was snowy-haired, sharp as a pin, and had a

2   Surrey History Centre, ref 2332

love affair with her dentist, according to her physiotherapist. Mrs Sherriff, bored with her husband's hobbies and craving escape from his physical demands, sounds like a good candidate for one of Alan Bennett's *Talking Heads* monologues. She worked in a local hospital for much of the First World War. When her boy became famous she would accompany him to California where she cooked him roast Sunday lunches in the blazing sunshine.

Beryl, Robert's sister, appeared on stage in two of his amateur plays written in the Twenties. She married a man called Tudor-Mash. His brother Bundy's life remains similarly obscure except for the existence of a short war diary he started in September 1917. He had initially joined the Royal Flying Corps but was rejected as unfit for flying and ended up in the Royal Berkshire regiment, serving in France without incident. Nobody now alive knew Robert well. His eulogy in 1975 was given by his Esher GP, Dr Dixon, who knew him only superficially and in later years.

Before World War One the Sherriffs were the classic, self-improving, hobby-loving, card-playing, patriotic family of Edwardian middle-England. They kept chickens, took the tram to the shops, ate fried sole once a week, and every year Robert re-read *The Diary of a Nobody* – a book close to home in its gentle mockery of suburban life. The annual holiday was in Bognor Regis, a ritual that was unvarying. In 1931 Sherriff published an internationally bestselling novel, *The Fortnight in September*. It's about the yearly ritual of the Stevens family of 22 Corunna Road, Dulwich. The family go to the seaside and after all sorts of deeply minor incidents they come home again. It is a superb evocation of the utterly ordinary and it was a huge bestseller in its day.

The modest but respectable circumstances of the Sherriffs were curiously similar to those of the Coward family living just a mile away in Teddington where Noël was born in 1899 when Robert was three. Their lives were oddly parallel. Robert and Noël went into the same officer training camp. They had West End hits at exactly the same time. Coward's spiritual home was the West End theatre and the Savoy Grill, whereas Sherriff was happy to stay put among the trimmed privet of outer London.

For a writer who chose public schoolboys as his subject, it comes as a surprise to find Sherriff didn't go to one. His father could not afford public school fees but he managed the ten pounds a term needed for Kingston Grammar School, founded in 1561 (though its roots go back to the 13th century). Its famous old boys include the historian Edward Gibbon and playwright Michael Frayn. The school back in 1900 had just sixty pupils and no playing fields of its own. It aspired, though, to the public school idea of 'muscular Christianity', an ideal epitomised by Rugby School and its Victorian headmaster Thomas Arnold, who while no sports maniac himself, invented an educational system that taught that Jesus was a virile team captain and God existed somewhere in the scrummage. It was a source of family pride that the Sherriffs were, according to a family history drawn up by a relative, descended from the Elizabethan grocer Lawrence Sheriff [sic] who founded Rugby School. Rugby (the setting of *Tom Brown's Schooldays*) was Sherriff's ideal. In *Journey's End* it becomes the fictional Barford where Raleigh and Stanhope were at school together.

There was no question of university. His father hadn't the money. Robert left school at seventeen and joined his father's world of insurance. It involved wearing a high stiff collar, a commute to Trafalgar Square on the train and then eight hours of filing and writing 'paid' against names in heavy ledgers. It was a career that should have ended in the late 1950s with a modest pension and a watch. When the war came, the eighteen year old saw it as his heaven-sent ticket out – along with half the country bored to death by their stultifying jobs.

Between August 1914 and December 1915, two and a half million men enlisted. It was the largest volunteer army ever seen and initially it took its officers from an approved list of public schools. Sherriff naturally wanted to be an officer. 'An officer, I realised, had to be a bit above the others, but I had had some experience of responsibility. I had been captain of games at school. I was fit and strong. I was surely one of the "suitable young men" they were calling for.'[3]

He was wrong. At his army interview the boy in front of him was from Winchester College. He was immediately accepted. Fully expecting the same treatment, Sherriff announced his school. The adjutant scanned the list. 'I'm sorry', he said. 'But our instructions are that all applicants for commissions must be selected from the recognised public schools, and yours is not among them.' And that was that.

The interview Sherriff described has been quoted in studies of the British army and its fast-changing sociology as it massively expanded. As the public schoolboys were wiped out (more officers were killed in the first few months of the war than in the previous 100 years put together) the army widened the net. Sherriff's rejection was illogical. In many ways he had the right education in that grammar schools were carbon copies of the public schools; lots of sport, Classics, prefect privileges, and a house system to encourage loyalty. As his own school was centuries older than many of the public schools on the army list, he had extra reason to be resentful.

Sherriff didn't leave his humiliating interview in a fury. That was not his style. He rationalised his rejection and was even, decades later, able to stick up for the army's logic in choosing officers the way it did. Looking back, he wrote: 'For the most part they came from modest homes, the sons of local lawyers, doctors, or schoolmasters… Pride in their schools would easily translate into pride for a regiment. Above all, without conceit or snobbery, they were conscious of a personal superiority that placed on their shoulders an obligation towards those less privileged than themselves.'[4] According to Sherriff the ranks liked them because these officers were 'young swells, and with few exceptions young swells delivered the goods.'[5] These were the

---

3   R.C.S., *Promise of Greatness*, p.136
4   Ibid., p.135
5   Ibid., p.154

sporty, modest, unswanking school types he would immortalise in his play.

In June 1915, Sherriff requested that Sun Insurance let him go. He was desperate to get into uniform. The company was already depleted and did not want to keep his place open, let alone pay his salary while he was at the Front. His boss commended his patriotic instinct but said no. So Sherriff left without permission.

In November 1915 he enlisted with the Artists Rifles, one of twenty-eight volunteer battalions that had combined to form the London Regiment before the war. The romantic-sounding outfit was formed in 1859 by painters, engravers and artists with Lord Leighton and John Millais leading the pack. Its headquarters were in Dukes Road, Bloomsbury and it recruited mostly graduates with a high number of musicians, actors, architects and newspapermen. By the time war broke out, the Artists had become an officer training corps and clearing house. Its men would be commissioned into other regiments. It had a terrible casualty rate. 6,000 of the 15,000 serving Artists would be killed, wounded or posted missing or captured. The Artists was Sherriff's first proper taste of military life.

Creatives in Khaki

In December 1915 Sherriff started his training in Essex, at Gidea Park, thirty minutes by train from Liverpool Street station. He spent most of January billeted on a family in nearby Romford. In March 1916 he moved into the grounds of Hare Hall Camp. The camp consisted of forty long wooden huts (fitted out by richer members of the Sportsman's Battalion whose first-class cricketers made the most of the grounds) that held 1,400 men in total. From a literary point of view Hare Hall was a major coincidence of burgeoning talent. Edward Thomas had arrived there in July 1915. At thirty-seven, he was a lot older than most recruits, a jobbing critic and a published author with a young family to support. He qualified as a lance corporal and a map-reading instructor. Another new face was that of Cadet Wilfred Owen (three years older than Sherriff) who arrived in mid-November before taking a commission in the Manchester Regiment six months later.

Owen and Thomas briefly shared a hut. But the meeting between them that should have happened never actually did. It is one of the great literary near misses of the 20th century. In his book *Strange Meetings*, Harry Ricketts invents an intriguing conversation in Hut 16 between Owen and Thomas. He doesn't, however, mention Sherriff who was ten huts away. Nor does Matthew Hollis in his recent book about Thomas, *Now All Roads Lead to France*. The reason no one has ever heard of Sherriff in connection with these men in training camp? He didn't go on to write poetry. Had he done so, however footling the verse, he would have been anthologized and discussed and his life story teased out over the years. But it was a poet's war and the playwrights have been ignored. One other thing: had Thomas, Owen and Sherriff met and then waited a year or two, they could have formed an army barbershop quartet with Cadet

Noël Coward. Coward's unhappy stint in the Artists ended when he caught a convenient virus and was invalided out with, he said, the score of Ivor Novello's *Arlette* running through his brain.

Owen, Thomas and Sherriff all experienced the same life of drill, more drill, further drill and occasional outings for some light shopping in Romford, the big excitement being the appearance of a Zeppelin. Judging from Sherriff's letters, the army life with the 'lunge-thrust-disembowel-disengage-two-three' of infantry training had scant appeal. Sherriff's martial spirit was always slightly lacking. His favourite lessons were map-making – it's tantalising to think that Edward Thomas could have been his instructor – at which he was extremely good. He learned how to reconnoitre, how to use a prismatic compass, how to find direction at night. The maps he left behind are sketched in a neat hand and done with great care. The Artists were red hot on the matter of turn-out and Sherriff spent a great deal of his time burnishing, brushing, crimping, oiling and buffing. He was once even ordered to polish a sergeant's bicycle with a piece of bacon.

There is a further, remote connection between Owen and Sherriff. He was Harold Monro, poet and proprietor of the famous Poetry Bookshop in Devonshire Street (now Boswell Street) in Bloomsbury. Monro was angry about the war ('how ungrudgingly Youth dies') before almost anyone else. In 1928 he would be at the first night of *Journey's End*. It was he who tipped off its eventual West End producer (his brother-in-law) that the play was a cracker.

At camp Sherriff was often homesick and lonely, though he re-met a friend from Kingston called Trimm 'whose only drawback is his extreme fondness for girls'. Why that should have been a drawback isn't clear. Sherriff's letters to his mother (he called her 'Dearie') are full of worries about appearing as miserable as he felt. It seems he had trouble joining in the singing and showing the required rowdiness of spirit. A devotee of the Stoics, he asked for a cheap edition of the *Discourses of*

Epictetus; it would accompany him months later to the Front along with Marcus Aurelius, Lewis Carroll and Walter Scott.

His letters to his mother are those of a bit of a mummy's boy whereas those to his father are upbeat and full of the utter absurdities of army life. For example, on 13 June 1916 he wrote to his father about training in Epping Forest: 'A Bombing Party consists of 2 bayonet men, 2 bombers, 2 carriers, 2 spare men and a commander. I put my rifle over the parapet of the trench, and the man on the other side throwing earth buried it. Luckily it was sand that came off fairly easily despite the fact that it looked like fried sole in egg and breadcrumbs. Made little seats to sit on and eat a sandy dinner. Then there was a raid. The experience would have been very pleasant bar the rain.'

He thought about joining the Royal Flying Corps but rejected the idea as it would have been a waste of months of infantry training. Sherriff's training finally came to a grateful end in late August 1916 and he took leave pending gazette. He was commissioned into his original choice of regiment, the East Surrey. Of the three budding writers at Hare Hall, only Sherriff would come back from the war: Edward Thomas would be killed by a shell blast in April 1917 and Owen machine gunned crossing a canal just a week before the Armistice.

The gentleman's outfitters Thresher & Glenny supplied Sherriff with trench coat, check cashmere jerkin and angora balaclava. He also took with him lots of anchovy paste and some decent wire cutters. He went to war wearing his tailored officer's tunic that the young Laurence Olivier would one day borrow and wear on stage. He set off from Charing Cross station, waved goodbye to his mother and vanished abroad on a boat train with hundreds of others doing the same, as if going off to school after the summer holidays. He noted a man next to him reading a paper with the optimistic headline 'Great Advance on the Somme, Thousands of Prisoners'. The troop ship arrived at Boulogne that afternoon.

The Gallants

The East Surrey Regiment was formed in 1881 and the 9th (Service) Battalion was raised in September 1914. The regimental depot was an easy walk from Sherriff's house in Kingston upon Thames. The men of the 9/East Surrey featured a lot of Londoners as the county back then included much of what is now suburban south London.

The battalion was just a pixel in the big composite picture of the Third Kitchener Army (K3). 2/Lt Robert Sherriff, just out of his teens, joined the battalion in the 72nd Brigade of the 24th Division and proudly stuck in his diary the picture of its stern commander, General Sir Henry Horne. The division had around 18,000 men in twelve battalions. A battalion had around 1,000 men including thirty officers. Each battalion was divided into four companies. Each company was subdivided into four platoons, each with four sections. Sherriff would end up in C Company, his surrogate family for his active service. This family would provide him his play's cast.

The men of the Division – mostly from south-east England – had joined up for a variety of motives: patriotism, joblessness, hunger, boredom. A fair few joined in preference to helping the police with their enquiries. Many were cockneys. Sherriff described them in his diary as 'a mob of several hundred civilians who had never touched a rifle in their lives…and surely never such a mixed crowd had been seen before: East End labourers: navvies: coalmen: shopmen: hawkers: burglars: I don't think a trade in London went unrepresented.'

The East Surrey Regiment could certainly not boast the same arty glamour as The Royal Welch Fusiliers, known as 'the literary regiment' because Robert Graves, Siegfried Sassoon, David Jones and so many other writers served in it. Graves in *Good-bye to All That* noted the snooty treatment meted out to an East Surrey officer on attachment to his regiment. But the

East Surrey could claim some future writers with theatrical and literary connections. Three years before Sherriff's runaway success with *Journey's End*, J. R. Ackerley (of the 8/East Surrey) caused a mini sensation in the London theatre. As a civilian Joe Ackerley was a mincing student nicknamed 'Girlie'. On the battlefield he proved an officer of true grit. He was wounded on the first day of the Somme. He recovered, returned to the front, again being wounded and then taken prisoner in 1917. His internment camp was a hotel in neutral Switzerland. There he set his play, *Prisoners of War*, during two weeks in July 1918. Somehow the censor failed to recognize it for what it really was – a gay play. Full of illicit yearnings and crushes, the pampered officers behave like schoolgirls. When the leading man Conrad strokes a young subaltern's head, the boy cries: 'Look out! Someone might come in!' Ackerley included lots of hysterics but sadly none of the pumping adrenaline of his own front line war experience.

Prisoners of War opened in 1925 and was considered 'morbid', a code word for queer. When the play was revived at the New End Theatre in London in 1994 it was reviewed very much as a forgotten landmark in the history of modern drama. It had nil influence on Sherriff who almost certainly never saw it. But its cast of upright officer types calling each other 'old man', their nerves shredded by the strains of war, is not dissimilar in tone. Nor is its language of the school dorm.

The other soon-to-be star of the East Surrey was the novelist Gilbert Frankau who wrote a hugely successful and very gripping 1920 war novel with the unmilitary title *Peter Jackson, Cigar Merchant*. It is virtually a history of the early days of the battalion and Sherriff's play is a sort of sequel to it. Frankau could not have been more different from Sherriff. He was a rich, dapper Old Etonian and a cracking snob, according to his fond grandson. He and Sherriff became friends. Gilbert's brother, Ronnie Frankau, was a comedian celebrated for his West End revue *Sauce Piquante* and their mother, Julia, wrote novels under the name Frank Danby and was a founder member of the Independent Theatre Club that did much to promote Ibsen, Shaw and serious drama in London. Now forgotten, Gilbert Frankau sold over a million books in his lifetime. He and Sherriff – briefly in the same battalion – were among the most commercially successful writers about the war.

The East Surrey was a good, tough regiment and it was famous for one legendary deed that massively boosted its media profile. On the fatal first day of the Somme, 1 July 1916, Captain Billie Nevill (of 8th Battalion) gave out four footballs and offered a prize to whichever platoon dribbled theirs to the German front line first. On one football was written: 'The Great European Cup-Tie Final. East Surreys v Bavarians. Kick off at zero. No referee.' The balls were duly dribbled toward the enemy frontline and Nevill – who was instantly killed – became a posthumous hero. The *Daily Mail* even got its house poet 'Touchstone' to write an embarrassing 'play up and play the game' ditty about the event in the manner of Henry Newbolt's cricketing poem 'Vitaï Lampada'. Quite what the Germans made of this act of sporting lunacy is not known. But for the British, World War One was always an away match. Their innocence was soon lost but the spirit of the sports field persisted and Sherriff's play would reflect it.

The narrative of the 9/East Surrey is actually part of the play – its history at the front climaxes in France shortly after the play ends. But even by the time Sherriff joined it the battalion had already been to hell and back. Its fiery baptism occurred almost exactly one year before he arrived in France, among the slag heaps in the mining district of Loos in late September 1915. Loos is a battle you find in anthologies of great military cock-ups. Its most famous casualty was Rudyard Kipling's son, the subject of David Haig's sorrowful play *My Boy Jack*.

Barely off the boat, soldiers with nil fighting experience were chucked into the battle after days without hot food, little sleep and soaking wet after endless marching. On the second day of the battle, of the 10,000 men ordered to attack 8,246 became casualties in under four hours. German casualties were nil. Those troops that made it to the enemy line, found the barbed wire unbroken and were soon picked off. Slaughter was followed by mass panic and retreat. The reputation of the 24th Division was unfairly trashed in this action and there was a great deal of buck passing by its commanders. Only the Germans spoke up for the British. They indicated to prisoners from the massacred 9/East Surrey (16 officers and 438 Other Ranks were casualties) their warmest admiration of the gallant advance of the Battalion. The battalion's nickname 'The Gallants' might be derived from this remark.

In *The Donkeys*, Alan Clark's bitingly sarcastic book about the slaughters of 1915, the British generals are savaged for their incompetence and Clark's account has set in stone the 'lions led by donkeys' theory. The lions were of course the men, the donkeys the generals. Sherriff, looking back on his unit's part in that hellish advance, wrote of it in his diary with a strong feeling for the hurt caused to volunteer pride that was totally characteristic of him:

Inexperienced officers and experienced NCOs were called upon to lead untried men through a dark night into the thick of a raging battle. They stood it finely for a while: then something failed; men lost touch and it is very obscure as to what happened. Some units, panic stricken, fell back, and the Division came out shattered by the loss of many of its best men, and worst still, with a branded name. 'The 24th? Oh yes, you mean the division that ran away at Loos.' You heard that expression everywhere. How the division won back its good name having unfairly lost it in an impossible test, stands as a splendid occurrence of the war.

After Loos, the battalion was rested and topped up, then spent the winter of 1915 in the Ypres Salient, the bulge in the line surrounded by the Germans, where they suffered constant casualties. Ypres ('Wipers') was referred to by Fred Billman, a corporal in Sherriff's battalion, as 'the city of the dead, the one place above all dreaded by soldiers.' During its six months in Ypres the battalion's casualties were light. The problem was more the weather, the trenches filling with water that turned to ice, causing frostbitten toes and much misery. From Ypres the battalion was moved to Wulverghem before arriving on the Somme in the summer of 1916. The Somme campaign was fought against better British judgment; it was explicitly designed to take the heat off the French who were suffering appallingly at Verdun. The first day (1 July) was an epic disaster for the British army with near on 60,000 casualties including 19,000 killed.[6] The Somme campaign dragged on until November.

For the 9/East Surrey there was terrible carnage during that summer. The fighting at Delville Wood, according to Sherriff, was 'a dreadful time where men fell like flies for no seeming gain.' Delville Wood was one of the 'untellable' battles of the war. It had the classic Great War horror landscape – shattered tree trunks, fuming shell craters, the ground thick with bodies and flies. The lowing of the wounded was its most ghastly feature. Every time the guns ceased the place was said to have sounded like a cattle ring at a Spring fair – an image used in *Oh What A Lovely War*.

To Sherriff, who arrived at the front a couple of weeks afterwards, the reports from the survivors must have been utterly terrifying. In August the battalion had lost nine officers and fifty-three Other Ranks, six officers and 175 Other Ranks wounded. By the end of the month the fighting strength was just 325 men. Sherriff was let in gently. On arrival in France he was sent to a 'cushy' part of the line, near Bruay. His first stay was at Base Camp in Étaples (or Eat apples). It was a depressing makeshift city of tents and hutments. Part of its function was to 'inculcate the offensive spirit.' Edmund Blunden in *Undertones of War* wrote about how a sergeant major was demonstrating the workings of a rifle grenade which then went off, killing him and everyone in

---

6   An even bloodier day was the Battle of Towton in 1461, featured in Shakespeare's *Henry VI Part 3*

the circle around him. Blunden only survived because he was loafing at the back.

The place was hated, the NCOs were brutal and Etaples was the scene of a minor mutiny, an incident dramatised by Alan Bleasdale for his 1986 BBC series *The Monocled Mutineer*, based on a book of the same name about the small-time crook and impostor Percy Toplis.[7] The series – with Paul McGann as the phony officer anti-hero – got good viewing figures and embraced all the cardinal First World War clichés: callous officers, utter futility and lashings of mud. Not to mention executions at dawn with a drunken firing squad puking at the horror of the task which they then botch. In dramatic portrayals of the First World War nothing ever goes to plan. Ever.

Sherriff's experience at Etaples was one of pure bewilderment. He felt like a new boy looking at the rules on the school notice board. Standing Orders had instructions on the proper saluting of French officers (due courtesy to the senior partner in a coalition force was strictly enforced) and on the prohibited shooting of rabbits and game. Shooting game was of course an on-leave activity for those officers lucky enough to have gamekeepers too old to fight. To some officers, Germans were partridges. The officer and poet-scholar Julian Grenfell actually entered the Pomeranians he shot in the game book at his family estate. He famously likened the war to a 'big picnic', which provided Bill Bryden with an ironic title for his 1994 Great War play.

The world of the front had elements of *Downton Abbey*. Sherriff's diary records that one servant was allotted to every three officers at a cost of two francs per officer per week 'for a short stay'. Sherriff's tailored uniform was deliberately designed to separate him from the men, his tunic and breeches conferring the army equivalent of 'upstairs' status. The Germans much appreciated this sartorial distinction as it made British officers easy to spot and pick off first in an attack. He was issued with

---

7   By William Allison and John Fairley, 1978

trench boots 'which would serve me many a good turn.' He liked the war best when it was most like his weekend rambles through the Surrey countryside.

In his diary he talks about various fellow officers including Blackman who was last seen hitting out at the enemy with a shovel on Vimy Ridge. Harding and High had previously been in the ranks and had then gone home to do officer training hoping the war would be over by the time they qualified. It hadn't, and now they were back. Percy High was in his late thirties, a kindly schoolmaster, like Osborne in *Journey's End*. 'Despite a certain abruptness of manner, I liked him instinctively from the first. He inspired confidence and his supply of shrewd common sense was enormous. He was a good companion,' Sherriff wrote in his diary. All the other officers were new to active service. On the subject of Etaples, Sherriff summed up its utter pointlessness: 'There was nothing to learn in this place about real war. There was only one place to learn that. You could only learn it in the trenches.'

His journey to the Front was a slow train via St Pol, where the men got their first taste of 'tray bon' egg and chips at a French estaminet. His diary contains a flash of literary purple as he heard the distant rumble of guns to the east. 'As I sat watching I realized that we were very nearly there at last, and that those green flickering lights shone over the very nucleus of the disturbance that had shaken the world...the Mecca of men from Ceylon, Australia and Canada – they came in thousands to die in stinking mud...'

Sherriff and his intake were to top up the numbers depleted by the Somme. He arrived six miles from the front line at the village of Estrée-Cauchy ('Extra-Cushy') where the 9/East Surrey had its HQ. There is a picture in his diary of a modest farmhouse. He met his commanding officer Lieutenant Clark, known as 'Nobby', a popular ex-colour sergeant whom Sherriff noted dropped his h's. The lopping off of aspirates to denote lower-class origins seems to be a common feature of trench dialogue in plays about the war.

As he walked into the mess an officer welcomed him with whisky. 'I accepted; as politeness suggested, but felt that 12 o'clock in the morning was hardly time for whisky – I felt so then because I knew nothing of the habits of active service.' In *Journey's End* Osborne welcomes the new boy Raleigh to the dugout with a large whisky and he accepts with the same bemusement. Whisky and the Western Front were inseparable for officers (the men were not allowed it although there was a rum ration in certain circumstances). Estrée-Cauchy also gave Sherriff his introduction to C Company. His first sight was a young officer, 'Father' Douglass, like 'Uncle' Osborne in the play a clergyman's son, drying a sock over a candle. The same sight (in the shape of Captain Hardy) opens *Journey's End*.

> Doubtless, there were other Companies as good, but C was mine and C remained mine during all the time I served in France and Belgium. By degrees, C Company became my most perfect ideal and it would have broken my heart to have been transferred to any other Company. C Company is an ugly, colourless expression, but it became a term of loving memory to me. We wore a red diamond of cloth above a green cross on our sleeves and the very sight of those colours brought a glow of pride to me. We had five different company commanders and twenty different officers while I was with the Company and my greatest pleasure to look back on is the fact that I remained with C Company all the time I was on Active Service. Everyday I became bound more surely to C Company and everyday I loved and esteemed it more.

Sherriff had arrived at the Front with Louis Abrams and Percy High. He now joined his other officers. Colonel Tew was in charge and Sherriff didn't like him one little bit. He drummed into the young officers new to the line their responsibilities. Sherriff left the briefing in a muck sweat. 'A cold dread came over me. "Am I an efficient officer" "Do I know enough" "Will I be sent back to England as an awful example of incompetence"', he put in his diary. The most memorable of the officers was

Captain Tetley, a far more genial man who had recently won the MC for rescuing men buried in a bombardment while under heavy shell-fire. The men adored him.

> He was the quickest tempered man I ever met, flying into a rage in the most childish way on the slightest provocation. He was the greatest object of amusement to the men and at the same time the greatest object of affection and admiration. In the line he was a marvel. Naturally highly strung and nervous, he was always with his men should there be any danger. Any shelling, any risky wiring to do, he was always there, and you could see what he suffered in nervous agitation. He would go round the line with a cheery word and joke with every man – then he would go down into his dugout and fly into a furious rage because a drop of water from the roof trickled down his neck.

Sherriff was never quite sure about the sarcastic Hilton, a man of jet-black humour whose response to any fatality was to cheerily shout: 'one further vacancy for a bright young thing in C Company!' Hilton clocked up a twenty-two-month stint in the trenches before being forcibly sent for rest by the Medical Officer and one wonders whether there isn't an element of him in the creation of Stanhope.

Nobby Clark was a more reassuring presence and part of the regular army from the old days – a career soldier – but he empathised with citizens in uniform like Sherriff. 'In the Mess Room he would talk with the most junior subaltern as if they were members of a village cricket team,' Sherriff wrote. (His play after *Journey's End*, *Badger's Green*, was all about a village cricket team.) It gave Sherriff a shock when he met the men he would be in charge of. Many had 'the look of the Somme' about them. Wilfred Owen had thought the men he saw at Etaples had a 'dead rabbit' face – a particular look no actor would ever be able to replicate on stage. Sherriff compared his men to Ali Baba's forty thieves, carrying parcels and ammunition belts and the clobber of war.

Sherriff and the others were to occupy a portion of the line at Vimy Ridge. On 2 October 1916 the battalion went into Divisional Reserve at the destroyed village of Souchez between Arras and Lens, his company being posted at a place called Cabaret-Rouge, now home to a large British war cemetery, then the reserve line to Vimy Ridge. The trenches zig-zagged from the Belgian coast right down to Switzerland. Although British accommodation never aspired to the wallpapered luxury of some German dugouts, it was in Sherriff's diary a smoky place of comfort, fruitcake, fried steak and tinned fruits.

I felt an immediate love for this dugout – with the spluttering candles making little shadows dance about the rough timbered roof, the steaming mugs of tea and the cheerful men who were becoming my friends; the feeling of fellowship (the herd instinct some would call it, I suppose) made the meal times in this little place the most looked forward to events of the day.

The officers' cook, Mason, in the play was drawn from life. Sherriff thought he was a hoot. His name was Morris (a fellow Thames-sider from Molesey) and he became a great feature of *Journey's End*. The actor Alexander Field played him at the stage premiere to guffaws at his cockney trench stereotype. His tea tastes of onions, his dishcloths are filthy, and his porridge lumpy. In inventing this character – a big feature of his diary – all Sherriff had to do was consult his memory. 'You never saw a more miserable man to look at: ill-fitting clothes, slouching walk, sleepy-looking blue eyes, and stubbly yellow hair – yet he never left the dugout without saying something funny.'

Sherriff records Morris's magnificent soliloquy about the rats' feast from the night before: 'what we do want is that bloke who hypnertised all the rats, and tootled them away wiv a flute, and took them all away into a mountain and shut them 'in – Hamilton was 'is name I think – I'd 'ave a try only I ain't got no flute, and there ain't no convenient mountain 'ere abouts – it 'ud be rotten to get them all out following yer and then not know what do wiv 'em? You can hear Morris's voice whenever Mason comes on stage. Morris/Mason is surely the immediate ancestor of the cheerful trench servant Baldrick in *Blackadder Goes Forth*.

One of Sherriff's first tasks in the line was the censoring of the men's letters home. This comes up early in his diary and it moved him greatly to read the crudely expressed but sincere letters from the men. He would use the business of letter censorship in his play.

There was something infinitely sad in those scrawled, thumb-soiled attempts from the men who never wrote letters before: from men who sought to tell wives or their mothers that no matter what happened they always thought of them and loved them. Some of those ugly little scrawls rang with a truer note than any elaborately worded missive could. A dirty bit of paper, no address, no date, – to Darling Jenny or Dearest Ma, telling her that he is well, hoping that she was the same… It is quite easy to laugh at the grammar, the crudities of spelling – the great big sprawling letters and the little 'i's for the first person singular; but when you see these notes before you and know the rough men who wrote them, when you feel with them; yearn, with them, for home; and suffer with them, there is nothing funny in these letters, they are things with a wonderful beauty.

When you see a great hulking man sitting on a box in the doorway of a mudhole dugout, with his head bent low over a dirty writing pad on his knee, working with a little stump of a pencil clenched in his great black fist as though he were carving the message out of a great lump of stone – when later, it is your duty to read that letter and you see written at the bottom – I am sending you a flower, give it to little Elsie and say Dad picked it orf the side of a trench – when you see things like that war ceases to be a brutalising force…

In his diary Sherriff wonders why he should have better quarters, better food, better clothing and more material comforts than the men. 'Perhaps it may sound terribly snobbish, absurdly conceited, yet I told myself that the average man in the ranks, who had no education – did not have these awful nameless fears. I told myself that whatever I enjoyed by way of better comfort, I paid out again in mental dread.'

His attempts to win over the men with informality caused him problems. This is a mistake Raleigh makes in the play when he feeds up top with the men, preferring their company to that of the other officers. Sherriff came to admit that the men were best left alone socially as 'most would prefer pack drill to being patronised.'

One of the assumptions about the war is that it was unremitting hell. But the truth is many men came home having experienced very little but acute boredom punctuated by moments of bowel-loosening terror as the odd speculative shell came their way. Even had they been exposed to fire there was in place a pretty guaranteed system of relief. Sherriff's experience in France would be that of every infantry unit – constant rotation between the firing line, the support line, reserve and billets. It was an almost unfailing system believed to have been the principal reason why British morale never cracked during the war. Any soldier could tick off the days (usually six) until he would be out of the line again. Sherriff, like most, thought of little else. He wrote in his diary: 'What an eternity of an evening this is! I think of the other hours of duty I have got to do – I shudder when I add them up: I shall never do it.' The play features his timetable in the single-scene first act.

Trotter: Six bloomin' eternal days. That's a hundred and forty-four hours… I'm going to draw a hundred and forty-four circles on a bit o' paper, and every hour I am going to black one in, that'll make the time go alright.

Stanhope: It's five to eight now. You better go and relieve Hibbert. Then you can come back at eleven o'clock and black in three of your bloody little circles.

'That Awful Affair'

J.R. Ackerley referred to his front line fear as 'the rabbit within.' The moment Sherriff arrived in France his war was a constant battle with his own inner rabbit. It was not just fear for his life, but fear that he would not be able to function properly as an officer. It fed directly into his play. The dread set in very early at Vimy Ridge and he never quite found a way of delousing himself of its effects.

On 10 October 1916 Sherriff's battalion relieved the Queens in trenches 300 yards from the front line on the edge of Vimy Ridge. Sherriff loathed the place: 'A sullen quiet lay over this valley of death. A brilliant summer was dying hard in a sultry autumn and there was an oppressiveness in the quietness.'

It was quiet, too damn quiet, he might have added.

From Estrée-Cauchy to the front line today takes just a few minutes by car. On foot back then it took several hours, down winding trenches, through the ruined village of Camblain-l'Abbé and on into flat country. It must have been an exhausting trek, the men loaded up with ammunition and supplies. The front line at Vimy ran roughly a mile parallel to the road that had once been the main route between Arras and Bethune. Here was the tiny HQ of C Company, the company that Sherriff remained with for the rest of his service and which he afterwards recreated on stage.

Company HQ measured nine by six feet. Bunks were constructed out of wooden frames and chicken wire and four layers of sandbags on the roof provided dubious protection. It was essentially an underground garden shed. Sherriff describes making his bed on a mackintosh in the corner, listening to the rain outside and dipping into *Meditations* by Marcus Aurelius, a book that he always had in his pocket. He was no intellectual but Sherriff never gave up his goal of self-improvement through the classics. The noble Roman was with him throughout his active service. His first few nights in the line he did his best to concentrate on sounds he liked – the upward rustle of flares and the sucking noises as an officer lit up his pipe. The Western Front was to newcomers like the first term at school – dangerous, strange, and with similar food.

No one going to the front by late 1916 did so with any illusions. Sherriff wrote in his diary: 'I had come to the war with no mad desire to do great things. I simply wanted to do well what I had to do: possibly I was a bit too imaginative to make a good soldier… I had heard the guns fire: I had heard the shells screech overhead. I had listened at night to the rattle of machine guns and I imagined the man behind the gun crouching in a sand bag emplacement and perhaps a German ration party on a distant road scurrying for safety. I had seen a little of the wreckage and enough of the wanton destruction of war to sicken me – and I had seen a little of how men lived and what men did in this queer land of give and take…the remainder I was to learn in the bitter, tasteless way that war has of teaching.'

On his first night in the front line Sherriff took a little tour of Ersatz Crater – a local feature – with a captain who would be killed by a shell some months later while marching his men to church. The very thought of the place would later make him shudder. He took a picture of the crater five years after the war and put it in his diary. It looks like a white fishpond surrounded by bullrushes and as innocent as you like. But here British and Germans exchanged as much 'hate' as they could muster. On the night of 9 October the crater was rushed by German Sturmkompanie – a vicious if minor retaliatory raid which left everyone decidedly 'windy.'

On 13 October the war diary records 'eight minneys fell around Ersatz Crater (some air bursts) and about 20 pineapples on left of Hartung trench. No damage done to our trenches.' Maybe no damage to the trenches but Sherriff and everyone else lived in fear of these fat shells. Minenwerfers were generally known as Minneys but also as oil cans, jam jars, Christmas puds. The large version was about the height and girth of a small man. Fired from a stubby trench mortar they were deployed where the opposing front lines were no more than 400 yards apart. Toffee apples – a bomb on a rod – exploded with a vicious bang. A whizzbang was a shell with a shallow trajectory, the whizz and the bang being almost simultaneous. Minneys were altogether different. Designed for the demolition of trench works they were a massive morale buster. A crude detecting system was in place where a minney sentry would spot a shell, study its trajectory and direct the avoidance tactics by use of hand signals and a whistle.

> Trotter: If you see a Minney coming – that's a big trench mortar-shell, you know – short for Minnywerfer – you see 'em come right out of the Boche trenches, right up in the air, then down, down, down; and you have to judge it and run like stink sometimes. (Act I)

Trotter wasn't joking. The shell visibly whooshed upwards like the stump of a pencil. Experienced soldiers knew that in normal circumstances you had about ten seconds between the crump of its launch and its impact on the ground. A hissing noise was sometimes discernible from inside the shell as it came down. The impact was a trench-quaking explosion of unbelievable volume, a spray of white-hot metal and then the sound of several tons of dirt and debris raining down. It left a crater several yards wide. A direct hit on a group of men would leave nothing to bury. Behind the lines, Miss Minnie Werfer was a popular turn in troop shows. In the line, however, the Tommies hated them. It was explained to me by a guide on a tour of Vimy Ridge that whenever British troops took a German trench and came across a surrendering Minney mortar crew they would kill them all instantly.

For Sherriff, the death of Private Chapman, killed by a Minney, was deeply shocking. The lad was in Sherriff's platoon.

The news had stunned me, when I heard it, I felt sick. Never before had death come so intimately, so close. A few hours ago, in the grey light of dawn, I had inspected my sections as they stood along the trench and now Chapman's face came vividly in my memory – it had been a stupid, boyish face with receding chin and watery eyes; he had stood there, with his rifle held for inspection and his face held down because a thin sprouting beard showed on his chin – and I had told him to shave the day before. I asked him why he had not done so, and he just shifted his feet about, stuttering something. Now he was dead – and I had worried him in his last hours.

Chapman had panicked and run under the shell. Only a leg was left of him, sticking in the ground. 'The sun soon dried the blood on the trench walls', wrote Sherriff in his diary. It was his job to write to the nineteen-year-old farm labourer's mother, living on a farm near Wisbech. He imagined the poor woman at home, a photograph of the boy on the mantelpiece.

But less violent life in the trenches formed the backbone of the *Journey's End*'s time-wasting ambience. Sherriff, for example, writes about an earwig running around the light of a candle. 'I thought what a fool the thing was, to spend its time running around a candle in a dugout on Vimy Ridge, when it was free to go anywhere. I sat and envied that earwig.' The earwig, soaked in whisky and put in a race, would become a conversational topic in the first act of the play. Sherriff records an incident in which an officer berates the cook for having no pepper (the last straw in a long day) and demands a runner be sent up the trench to fetch some from another mess. Again, in *Journey's End* a furious demand for the missing pepper is a little detail that reveals some more serious emotional deprivation. 'War's bad enough *with* pepper – but without pepper – it's – it's bloody awful', says Trotter in Act I.

Vimy is described with close attention to the hushed tension of the front line. In those first days, Sherriff describes going up to within thirty yards of the German line. This was heart-stoppingly close. The rustle of his macintosh on corrugated iron, the whispers of the sentries, the hushed 'alright thankee, sir' of a seasoned sergeant returning the nervous officer's enquiry, all made a huge impact on him. Even when it was 'all quiet' along this long and meandering British line, he noted that men were still dying at a rate of twenty an hour. These were often totally random deaths. His description of Private Smith going to fetch some wood for a trench revetment, being diverted momentarily by the beauty of the sunset (a spot of artistic embellishment possibly?) and in that very instant being caught by a sniper, produces some nice laconic writing in his diary. 'The men stand round stupidly, then one takes hold of Smith's shoulder and awkwardly turns him over. 'Been 'it, mate?' he says – which was the last and stupidest thing ever said to Smith.'

What emerges from his diary and letters is that Sherriff's days at Vimy were the death of any idea that he would emerge from the war as a hero, a notion he might have entertained in his dreams back in Hampton Wick. His misery worsened at the thought that his fear was somehow lower-class. Innate courage, he seemed to think, came more naturally to public school boys. The distinction now sounds ridiculous but it was real enough to him. Sherriff bemoaned the lot of the junior officer in his diary:

> The platoon commander held personal responsibilities that would have made an Army Commander shudder. An Army Commander may make a mistake and a thousand men may die. He may know none of these men – he has probably seen none of them: they died miles away from him. It can be no worse for him than a farmer who orders a dozen cockerels to be killed.

> But a Platoon Commander may make a mistake and he sees dozens of men die; men who he has known for months, so well they are personal friends. He sees their wax-like faces, and their great glazing eyes looking at him – these men he had cared for as best he could – he sees them squirm in agony: shriek in pain – because he made a mistake. So

this responsibility came to me for the first time. I looked across the valley and saw the Minneys crashing down – I saw huge clods of earth tossing about: a sheet of corrugated iron bounced up in the air sideways, and came floating down flatly in the wind. Should I go on, or wait?

The gradual realisation that he was not quite officer material was taking over his life.

If you are to date the start of his decline, it is in the battalion's brief stint at Vimy. It earns a key reference in *Journey's End*. In his cups Stanhope confides to Osborne that it was 'That awful affair on Vimy Ridge. I knew I'd go mad if I didn't break the strain. I couldn't bear being fully conscious all the time… There were two ways of breaking the strain. One was pretending I was ill – and going home. The other was this *(he holds up the glass)*.' (Act I)

Sherriff never drank much. But in the play, Stanhope's dependence on booze probably started at Vimy. This was certainly the opinion of the cast in the 2004 production. There is nothing especially dramatic I could find that happened to the battalion that would have justified Stanhope's description of 'an awful affair.' But for Sherriff it was the onset of a crisis of nerve that never left him while he was in the line. From Vimy onwards his war was all about fear-containment. He obsessively studied the duty roster – recreated in his diary in a neat little timetable – 'noting the times when I should be exposed to death on the Ridge.'

Sherriff's nightmare could have been any of several instances of horror. The crater raid was just one of them. The back of a private's head was blown off, a very distressing sight for everyone. After the inevitable counter-attack, the officer returned to the dugout. In his diary, Sherrif writes: 'Penrose stopped and no one said a word; a servant came and silently cleared the breakfast things – but Penrose still sat at the table, twisting a piece of paper.' It reads like a stage direction.

He also cites the example of a machine gunner who was looking across no-man's-land, humming a tune, when a sniper shot him between the eyes. The next day he found the dead man's helmet, full of matted hair and blood. Sherriff was appalled by these killings and records the commanding officer's platitudinous response: 'He was a good man – and an old hand at the game.'

Sherriff goes on to describe another man, during a barrage, buried up to his shoulders in the earth while his mates furiously tried to dig him out. The man couldn't move his arms to cover his face and the shelling was so bad the men were repeatedly forced to retire. Eventually it was safe enough to bring him in. He was in one piece but when they laid him out on the fire-step he died of shock. Sherriff wrote these grisly happenings down so as to give some idea of the toll of the war.

His first night on duty he was responsible for 100 yards of British line for three hours. His wrote that his watch hands hardly seemed to move it was so tense. There was no shortage of nastiness to justify his fears. On his last day at Vimy Ridge he recalled in his diary an incident about a well-liked corporal who had woken in his sleep and started wandering up and down the trench, groping his way along and murmuring to himself like Lady Macbeth. The men couldn't get him to snap out of it. Sherriff went along to find out what state the corporal was in. The man had gone insane. 'What an infinite world of suffering it must have meant,' he wrote. 'What a little tragedy it really was: a sane man losing his reason, suddenly, quietly in a moonlit trench.'

The journey out of the line for Sherriff was paradise. He wrote of the sheer relief as the men made their way to safety through meadows. 'To walk upright and not be shelled – to sing out loud and not be sniped – is it not a joy – an unspeakable joy?' He was not overdoing it. Sherriff started Scott's novel *Guy Mannering*. 'Books are splendid things when you are lonely and I loved my little blue leather books of Scott that I had with me.' Sherriff again mentions reading Plato, Marcus Aurelius ('quite an old friend by now') and Epictetus. None of them did him as much good as *Alice in Wonderland* – 'the finest book ever written.' His love for Lewis Carroll he passed on to Osborne in the play. He recites from 'The Walrus and the Carpenter' minutes before his death. Alice is there, too, in the screenplay he wrote for the 1942 film *Mrs. Miniver*. Greer Garson reads the book aloud to her children during an air raid as a diversion from their fear. Sherriff was one of several uncredited co-writers but the scene is unmistakably his work.

Sherriff admitted that after a month in the trenches he had yet to see the worst war had to offer. He even considered joining the Flying Corps to escape the infantry. A galloping fear of shells is a constant in almost everything he wrote privately during the war. To his father he wrote a letter (5 October) with a comforting mathematical formula. 'When I hear 6 shells go off together I think there are now only x-6 shells to be fired (to use an algebraic expression) before the war ends, so when x-x shells have been fired war is bound to end – I have not suddenly gone mad – but this is a thing to cheer you up when you hear shell after shell whizzing over head.'

He could not get used to it. 'What I hate is the suspense of waiting for these shells to come down and when they are up in the air the excitement of running along to judge their fall takes away the fear for a minute – it is after the explosion that you feel cold and frightened all over – and then is the time you have got to smile to reassure the men.' The day he wrote that letter, 14 October, was the day Hilton had sent him into no-man's-land to inspect some wiring with a corporal. In October T. H. S. Swanton took over as CO, replacing the injured Colonel Tew who had been crushed by his own horse, much to Sherriff's relief. Colonel Swanton was worse. At just twenty-eight, he was a career army officer and a martinet.

At around this time Sherriff took delivery of a 'body shield' (a banned item technically). He fired a few rounds from his revolver to test it out. It worked well. He didn't want the men to see him wearing it, as it would have seemed unfair. But he vowed to keep it handy if the time ever came when he had to go over the top. His thoughts about the Flying Corps waned a little. He worried that 'I was simply seeking to escape from a danger I cannot face.'

Troglodyte

At the end of October, Sherriff got news that altered his career for the better in France. He and fifteen men were to proceed to Mazingarbe to join the 254th Tunnelling Company, Royal Engineers. It was a world of underground passages, listening galleries, stethoscopes and spoil duties – all part of the front's unseen subterranean war, the sort Sebastian Faulks brilliantly recreates in his novel *Birdsong*. It was the start of the happiest two months of his active service and it was spent in the Loos salient with its 'quiet, mysterious, romantic charm.' The men sent with him were pretty useless. In his diary Sherriff recorded the moment when the Captain asked the Sergeant Major who should be sent:

– "Johnson, for one, sir, we can't do nothing with him."

– "Now who else?"

– "We better get rid of Birtles and Wooley, sir, they are absolute wasters."

– "Alright, Birtles and Wooley", says the Captain writing them down.

– "Now, one more, Sergeant-Major."

The Sergeant-Major stands deep in thought – the chance is absolutely too good to miss.

– "Preston is an awful fool, sir." – he says at last.

– "Send Preston then…warn them will you, Sergeant Major?"

– "That I will, sir", he says chuckling with delight.

Thus Sherriff ended up with 'open-mouthed wretches with weak intellects' as he charmingly called them. The tunnelling party amounted to two officers and sixty men. They came to Vermelles, a village that in 1914 had been horribly martyred being so close to the front line. Men fought in its front gardens, cabbage patches, cellars and sheds, up and down the main street, chucking bombs from bedroom windows, dying on sofas, in kitchens and greenhouses.

Sherriff surveyed its ruins as he made his way to the chateau. He ended up in La Rutoire trench, the most famous communication trench in France. The war's equivalent of the M4, it was 3,700 yards long and beautifully dug into deep white chalk. It had not one single dugout the whole of its length and was consequently nearly always deserted. Sherriff and his men plodded down it. Then came the sound of shells. 'How I hated and loathed that sound! – that crash – that whine of flying metal.'

Eventually he arrived at Hay Alley, a trench that led into the Loos Salient, just before the village of Hulluch. He hung up his gas satchel in a dugout that would be his home for two months. He was about half a mile from the front line. It was here that he started his duties in charge of the spoils party, lugging chalk from the mining system. As an officer, he did no lugging himself of course. The tunnellers were near a trench called Ninth Avenue, beneath forty feet of solid chalk. The spoil was taken by cart to the foot of the steps into the mine, the bags dragged up and it was then Sherriff's job to see the bags emptied into shell holes, all of this under cover of night. The white spoil was then carefully covered over to keep it from view of enemy aircraft. According to his diary, the work was a mixed blessing.

Oh! But the infantry private had a deadly, sordid, wretched, heartbreaking job! Can you imagine it? Eight hours – ceaseless hours of groping in the dark on a barren plain…after eight hours they go back and sleep in holes where stinking water drips on them and rats and filth and lice torment them. They sleep as best they can: eat their rations, sleep again, and get up and go to work once more. Day in day out, for weeks and weeks: yet they clung to this job lovingly when they thought of the front line.

He was in the tunnels for nine weeks, from 25 October to 28 December 1916. He had a privacy he hadn't known since he joined the army. He also felt much safer. On 16 November he wrote home that he would do 'anything in preference to that waiting and waiting that characterises the infantryman's work. ... I would far sooner be one of the miners picking away all the time they are on duty than do the work of any infantryman.'

One of the pleasures of his new assignment was a walk into Mazingarbe in the company of the ever-chipper servant Morris down a route he compared to the Cromwell Road in London. The calm was shattered when on his return he found sixty East Surrey men and two officers to help work on the mines. The upside was that Sherriff was reunited with Patterson, an officer he had met in Cabaret Rouge and spent forty-eight terrifying hours with on Vimy. Much of the remaining section of his diary (it ends at Christmas 1916) is taken up with tales of 'Pat' Patterson and his fellow officers Gibson and James. Because the line was quiet there, neither side did anything more than intermittently exchange fire in the occasional 'hate.' Sherriff mentions working with Moyes, a professional engineer who he was delighted to find was a keen antiquary and a descendant of Sir Walter Scott. He was extremely sympathetic and a good listener. But Sherriff noticed in his diary that Moyes was not well. Wounded at Ypres, he had been in the line too long and his nerves were shattered: 'he cannot go sick because there is nothing outwardly wrong with him: his health is perfect physically so he has to go on,' Sherriff lamented in his diary. 'Every little while you can see he is listening for some unseen, nameless terror.... No one can possibly think less of Moyes for his dreadful fears.'

The 9/East Surreys took up residence in the front line at Hulluch on 12 November. The war diary records aerial darts, rifle grenades, rum jars, whizzbangs, and an enemy machine gun 'playing about.' Sherriff was not free of the odd crisis. A shell fell behind the dugout and left him unable to eat a thing. He wrote to his mother on 12 November: 'I am afraid I am more nervous than the average because I certainly feel the shock of these sudden dangers more than the average.' The next day he was only able to write in note form about his fear: 'shell whizzes over...feel sick – breathing comes hard heart beats. NERVES.'

He worried, too, that applying for a transfer to the Engineers would irritate his CO with whom he was already in trouble because of the dirty appearance of his men. He considered joining the Royal Engineers full-time. He made an application and the Colonel reluctantly signed it. Officers were in short supply and too many men wanted to leave the squalor of infantry life. For weeks he cherished the idea of a transfer, reading up everything he could on tunnelling, which he found fascinating.

By the end of the month his mind was on the Christmas holiday and how he used to look forward to the 'day of days' (Christmas Eve) when he would walk back from school and watch the shops still being decorated. He reminded his mother of their trip to the theatre to see *Nell Gwynne*. Casualties for the battalion in November were three privates killed, thirteen wounded.

The cold in December was lung-numbing. The men were living like tramps in ditches. Although hot food was more plentiful, fires were not permitted. At night he wore his vest, shirt, leather jacket, woollen jersey, fleece lining, scarf and cap comforter in a sleeping bag with two mackintoshes over him. On one occasion he asked his servant to serve him his breakfast in bed. He kept warm by walking along the trenches. The meagre warmth from the dawn sunshine was bliss. He writes about lice. These horrible translucent little lobsters were an itching hell, a bad infestation unendurable. The men 'strafed' them with special lice powder or ran a candle along the seams of their clothing. Lice could make troops suicidal.

Sherriff was officially reprimanded by the adjutant for the poor appearance of his men. He was being too wet with them. 'When it is my power to make the men's time easier I love to do so as the poor men have such a hard time usually, he wrote home on 1 December. He said how much he hated 'nigger driving' and the incessant nagging and punishment that was required to get the men to spruce up. Sherriff noted that the new colonel shouted at one offender – 'if you're not out of my sight in half a second I'll have you strangled.' The war caused a constantly shifting mood. 'At one moment this romance and glory of war would sing its wonderful songs to you. At the next moment the sordid wretchedness of war would shriek at you and leave you crushed, crushed with hopeless depression,' he wrote in his diary.

The battalion when he returned to it was having not much festive fun. 23 December the war diary records as – 'A lively day. Enemy continually bombarded our front & support lines & Btn HQ with whizz-bangs, 4.2s, and tear shells. Sent over innumerable darts and about 100 Minneys.' Casualties were 'light' – 11 men were wounded, one killed. On Christmas Eve four men were killed by 'Hun artillery' having just received letters from home wishing them a Happy Christmas. A shell landed in a crowded communication trench. One man from D Company had his head blown off.

The battalion – which had suffered two cases of accidentally self-inflicted wounds and a suicide – was under strain. They had a concert party staged by B & D Companies with a trio of officers singing a spoof version of 'Another little drink won't do us any harm.' Sherriff had already experienced Tetley's singing, which he found 'screamingly funny because it was so feeble.' Sherriff spent Christmas with the Royal Engineers. He wrote out the special menu in his diary that was devised by master-chef Morris. It started with Consommé Turtle, followed by Boeuf braisé aux tomates legumes, Pudding a l'Anglais, Coquillages à la Russe, then fruits and coffee. A hole was bored through the dugout walls and into the kitchen. A string was tied to one end and in the kitchen on the other end was attached a tin with an apricot stone in it. When the bellrope was pulled, the stone rattled the tin and in came Morris with the next course. Morris played along and served with exaggerated dignity. The officers decided the turtle had eaten nothing but celery all its life, that the watery sauce accompanying the beef would have been better served as drink, and that the pudding looked as though it had been dropped from a great height. The coquillage was meat paste on tiny bits of toast. Cherry brandy was served with the coffee. Morris was, however, roundly congratulated and proud as punch. Christmas Eve 1916 ended to the crump of guns. Everyone's nerves were on edge, sniffing the air for gas and watching the sky for red and green rockets. The war diary summed it up as 'the best possible Xmas under the circumstances.'

28 December was Sherriff's last day as a temporary tunneller. He returned to the battalion billets in La Philosophe with a lump in his throat. His permanent transfer had been denied. In the New Year he hankered for a spell of leave but knew there was a queue ahead of officers waiting their turn. The MO was busy with cases of trench foot. The weather turned extremely cold early in the New Year. The shelling on New Year's Day was dreadful. The enemy sent over minneys, gas shells and whizz-bangs. The barrage killed six men with four wounded. Again, you hear in Sherriff's letters the sound of an imminent crack-up. 'I think the longer one has in the line the nervier one gets – there is no "getting used to it" I am afraid, it is simply bearing it,' he wrote home on 21 January. By the end of the month he again wrote home about neuralgia around his left eye. He felt a fraud for being in a rest station, thinking it 'very mean', his problem being so trivial while his men were in the trenches.

Things had got so bad with the neuralgia that on 27 January he was admitted to a dressing station where he was kept under observation. A Field Medical Card, stamped 17 Field Ambulance, reads 'Neuralgia affecting the eyes.' He wrote to his mother two days later, 'As yet I can't get the thought of going up the line out of my head – it seems the farther away from it you are the more it preys on my mind and I feel I simply CAN'T go up again.' He was deeply guilty about his condition. No doubt the pain was real but the cause was probably psychological. His brother officers must surely have wondered among themselves about the nature of his illness. Was he perceived as a frightful funk? If so, no one commented.

Gingering Fritzy

On 23 January the Germans launched an attack that was successfully fought off. Two days later the 9/East Surrey retaliated with a bigger raid, carried out by A Company. Sherriff would write a raid into his play with some interesting parallels. Raids by early 1917 were all the rage and known as 'winter sports'. The contemporary doctrine was that raids were serious, useful, necessary operations of war. They were designed to keep everyone busy, on the offensive, and to dent enemy morale. They were even relished by some as a chance to win medals. They were of course incredibly dangerous, particularly to those doing the raiding. In the first seven months of 1916 almost 6,000 men died and 120,000 were wounded on raids.

The raid by the 9/East Surrey was hugely successful and conducted, most unusually, in broad daylight. At midday three officers, fifty men plus half a dozen sappers went over the bags. The men sprinted 100 yards across no-man's-land under cover of smoke, mortar and Lewis gun fire, through the enemy wire where gaps had been blown by artillery. The Germans were not quick enough off the mark. In command were 2/Lt Thomas ('Tommy the Bomber') and Sergeant Summers, both famous in the battalion for their love of danger. 'Lizzie' Lindsay was the third officer. They bombed, shot and bayoneted every Boche in sight before returning with their prizes just ten minutes later.

The raid produced three prisoners, one gas helmet and a sample of ration bread (so as to assess the quality of enemy rations in the 'Turnip Winter' of 1917). The raiding party lost three killed and four wounded; the Germans lost around twenty men. The raid was considered a huge feather in the battalion's cap and the three officers were among those later decorated. General Horne passed on his congratulations. The raid did exactly what all such raids were designed to do: extract information, inflict enemy casualties and, in army parlance, give Fritzy a gingering.

In *Journey's End* the raid becomes something else. It is a dreadful tragedy. It occurs before dusk under cover of smoke and through a single hole that's been blown in the German wire. It's clearly suicidal given its lack of surprise. Stanhope points out that with just one hole blown in the wire the Germans will have a dozen machine guns trained on it. 'Why didn't the trench mortars blow a dozen holes in different places – so the Boche wouldn't know which we were going to use?' he asks the Colonel. (Act III, 1) Stanhope doesn't object to the raid per se but he does protest at the lack of adequate planning and the need to have the raid report prepared in time for dinner further up the chain of command.

Osborne and Raleigh brace themselves for the task – a sixty-yard dash into a trench full of Germans ready and waiting. Then there's the scene, the play's most famous, in which Osborne, having given his wedding ring to Stanhope 'just in case', kills the time before going over the top in chat with Raleigh, the older man desperately trying to be positive, clearly aware that neither of them is likely to make it back. Osborne breaks into verse: 'The time has come the walrus said, / To talk of many things.' A joint rendition of Lewis Carroll is followed by a discussion of the joys of Lyndhurst and the New Forest, a knowledge of which both men have in common. The minutes tick by to the moment when they must go over the top. As they approach the steps, Mason says, 'good luck Mr Raleigh.'

The raid is dealt with through sound effects. A stage direction provides a little descriptive essay of the various noises off from no-man's-land as the enemy wakes up to the raid, sends up alarm rockets and chucks bombs. A boy from the 20/Wurtmebergers is snatched and brought back. The colonel is thrilled and forgets to ask about casualties, adding too late: 'Oh – er – what about the raiding party – are they all safely back?' To which Stanhope coldly replies: 'Did you expect them to be all safely back, Sir?' (Act III, 1)

The cost of this raid is seven British lives. The Colonel tells Stanhope how pleased the Brigadier will be. Stanhope, mourning his friend Osborne, replies with sarcasm: 'How awfully nice – if the Brigadier's pleased.' Raleigh, numb and bleeding, returns to the dugout speechless at his first sight of death (in a past production he was covered in someone else's blood) and sits down. Stanhope then delivers what is the play's most famous line – 'Must you sit on Osborne's bed?' The curtain comes down on the scene. (Act III, 2)

Alan Napier saw Laurence Olivier play Stanhope. 'The thing that Olivier's always been able to do is to etch certain lines that ring in your head until the day you die.' He was referring to the line about Osborne's bed. 'A simple line,' said Napier, 'but it displayed the whole agony of war in the trenches and your best friend dying before your eyes – I can hear it to this day.'[8]

The actor saying it has a lot of leeway. The line is both a reprimand, a plea or both. In the 2004 production Stanhope slowly goes through Osborne's effects – his pipe, his watch, his ring – looking at them one by one as the loss of his friend sinks in. In Sherriff's mind the association of the trench was always with the school dorm even though he never boarded. For so many homesick young officers, the trenches were an extension of the school experience. Sherriff wrote to his mother on 29 January and lamented a return of the Sunday night blues. 'I feel extremely like the time when I did not want to go to school and worked up a worried expression and said I felt sick, etc., but now, in a greater sense I feel the same thing – nothing bodily wrong – only a great mental tiredness...'

The raid preceded a very quiet February. Having completed their tour in the Hulluch-Lens sector, the 9/East Surrey was relieved. On 12 February they moved into a training area five miles west of Béthune where they practised bombing and shooting. It was then on the march to Bas Rieux where the regimental boxing match took place at the local school. That month fourteen men were wounded and one killed in action.

---

8   Quoted in *James Whale* by James Curtis, p.22

The war diary records that a few 'injudicious Huns' wandering about were snipered.

In March the battalion was in the Calonne area. Alongside the front line was a slagheap that continuously smoked and was known as 'Burning Byng' after the general 'Bungo' Byng. At Bully-Grenay C Company was given wiring duties. By mid-month the battalion was back in the line. Enemy pineapples and whizz-bangs searched for what the war diary wonderfully calls 'our flying pig emplacement.' At night, rockets lit up the sky. Aeroplanes on either side buzzed around zinc skies, occasionally dropping low for a strafe. Sherriff became Mess President, his job to provision the dugout, do the accounts and extract subscriptions. At the end of March he was photographed at Bully Grenay, looking pretty haggard alongside six other members of C Company including Lt Douglass, 2/Lt Trenchard and Capt. Godfrey Warre-Dymond. In a *Sunday Times* interview (an interview with almost no quotes) by George Perry, Sherriff admitted that Warre-Dymond 'bore more than a close resemblance to Stanhope in the play.'[9] We'll come to him.

Of the other men he was photographed with, tubby-looking Cecil Trenchard was a former stockman in Australia. He was wounded in April 1917, losing an eye, which ended his war. He was partly the role model for the excellent Trotter, the food-obsessed ex-ranker officer. Rubbing his tummy, he was a hugely popular figure with audiences in early productions of the play. 'Father' Douglass is – along with Percy High – in part 'Uncle' Osborne, the quiet intelligent schoolmaster who once played rugby for England, the moral compass of the play and Stanhope's close confidant. Archie Douglass survived the Somme but died of wounds in April 1918 at the age of thirty. Sherriff thought he was fantastic and wrote in his diary:

> He was a man of few words. He hated affectation and hated vulgarity. He would sit for an hour or more at a Mess table, without saying a word, smoking cigarettes that dangled from

---

9   *Sunday Times* Magazine, 16 April 1972

his upper lip – leaning forward and occasionally chuckling to himself at something that amused him. He was about the coolest man I ever saw in the trenches.

Jimmy Raleigh – naïve, young and idolising – has no counterpart except perhaps in Sherriff's imagination. He is a cypher – a portrait of public school cricket-happy eagerness and decency, the most upper-class of the characters and with army connections. He is the hardest part for an actor to flesh out in the play. 'The Germans are really quite decent, aren't they? I mean, outside the newspapers?' he says. Osborne replies with a story about a decent German officer who fired up flares to help some Tommies carry a wounded comrade back from no-man's-land at night.

Raleigh: How topping!

Osborne: The next day we blew each other's trenches to blazes.

Raleigh: It all seems rather – silly, docsn't it? (Act II, 1)

Quite how these minute criticisms of the war allowed the play to be seen as a major pacifist statement, is a puzzle. Perhaps the gung-ho-ness of much Twenties war literature made *Journey's End* seem sensitive and thoughtful by comparison. The play was certainly free of the recruiting poster sentiments that Sherriff might have written had he not been in action and seen the reality.

A Blasted Funk

One thing is for sure. Sherriff mentally went downhill in the spring of 1917. His life was ruined by incoming shells, shells yet to be fired, shells that had nearly missed, the shell with his number on it. Nothing could relieve his neuralgia except an escape from the shelling. He kept it to himself in the line. But the tone of his letters is desperate. 'I feel I would be willing to do anything – resign my commission and work at any kind of work as long as I am only away from the awful crash of explosions which sometimes quite numb me,' he wrote home on 1 February.

The weather didn't help. It was snowy. He wrote a short story called *The Cellars of the Cite Calonne*, his theme being an evening spent with his comrades in good cheer. It was followed by a welcome stint behind the lines training recruits for a fortnight in March. He was back with the battalion on 24 March. The Battle of Arras opened on 9 April with the Canadians storming Vimy Ridge, forcing an urgent retreat by the Germans from the Lens salient. The city was massively hit with gas shells and the 9/East Surrey took over a new front line on 16 April on the outskirts of the town.

Sherriff had reached rock bottom. 'It is funny that when I get a return of this I always get a return of this nervousness again...it is such a trial specially when you have to conceal it from the men,' he wrote to his mother on 2 April. Five days later his neuralgia was again bad. 'I always get this when I get near the guns again, but I am always hoping it will get better in time.' It didn't. On 14 April he wrote to his father, 'I absolutely could not bring myself to face the line again and I went to a doctor and explained everything to him, he has given me a few days rest at the transport.' On April 17 he again wrote to his father: 'Naturally doctors are suspicious of these kind of cases as there are no doubt many who try this on... He examined me and said there was no question as to my nervousness and asked if I could think of any reason for it...'. The doctor prescribed Sherriff some tablets and asked him to come back later. 'I am absolutely in his hands – if he decides I am fit to go up the line I must go – but what I dread is that by going up I should make some serious mistake through lack of confidence.'

Earlier that year, Wilfred Owen sent a letter to his mother. 'I can see no excuse for deceiving you about these last four days. I have suffered seventh hell', he wrote after being shelled for fifty hours continually.[10] During the bombardment the water in his trench rose above his knees and Owen says he nearly gave up and let himself drown in it. Sherriff, too, was very near the end of his tether. He would go to bed reading Marcus Aurelius who told him 'nothing happens to any man which he is not formed by nature to bear.' All very well but Marcus Aurelius had never been shelled.

Shell shock was still not a diagnosis that Sherriff ever considered or aired. 'The suspense of long hours of duty in the line tells upon you... I think nearly everyone gets to this state sooner or later and it is of course a question of their powers of being able to conceal their fear after that', he wrote to his father on 17 April.

Stanhope is a true to life portrait of the wreckage done by too long in the trenches. He drinks not to evade his responsibilities but so that he is better able to perform them. He is a functioning wreck. Max Hastings in his book *Bomber Command* writes about Guy Gibson VC, twenty-five-year-old leader of the Dam Busters: 'Not a cerebral man, he represented the apogee of the pre-war English public schoolboy, the perpetual team captain, of unshakeable courage and dedication to duty, impatient of those who could not meet his exceptional standards.'[11] No wonder Sherriff was later drawn to the film of the Dam Busters story. Gibson was like Stanhope minus the drink.

---

10   Letter 16 January 1917, *Owen: Collected Letters* by Wilfred Owen
11   Max Hasting, *Bomber Command*, p.256

There were men of the 9/East Surrey raid who seemed to like danger, Summers and Thomas for example, and were in their own way freaks. But even the bravest were prone to tears, booze, and, like Stanhope, morbidity. Stanhope complains that when Trotter sees a trench wall he just sees a brown surface. 'He doesn't see into the earth beyond – the worms wandering about the stones and roots of trees.' But maybe what Stanhope sees is the inside of a grave, his mind moving through the earth like fish through water. Body parts were always cropping up in trench walls. The frontline was a vast ossuary. Immediately following that chilling thought, Stanhope orders a bottle of whisky.

Despite the lavish praise of Stanhope in the play by Osborne, both Osborne and Trotter would arguably have been better company commanders by the time the play opens. The actor playing Stanhope is playing an alcoholic martinet who is at the edge of reason. He nobbles the battalion doctor; he threatens a junior officer with his gun, and he talks gibberish. While the army was suspicious of psychiatric problems, good COs were not blind to men who were near cracking point and needed a break. Sherriff refers in his diary Louis Abrams ('Abey' from Trinidad), a young officer he arrived in France with, and whom he mentions as continually drinking whisky. It turns out that Abrams had a breakdown and went Absent Without Leave in early 1917. He was court-martialled and cashiered but treated leniently and sent home to Trinidad. It was a fate that Sherriff may have half-envied.

Quite what impact he made on those around him is unclear. Did his other men spot his crisis? The Battalion was getting a break from the front line and on 25 April he wrote to his father again about his neuralgia: '...the doctor I had been visiting thought it may be due to a straining of the eye muscles – I don't care what it is if only someone can cure it for me. The trouble is it comes on for about an hour two or three times a day and while it is on it makes me feel absolutely knotted up – when it is over I feel quite fit again.'

In early May 1917 Sherriff's battalion marched to Lozinghem, the column showing off to the French villagers all the German trophies they had captured. Early May produced a huge burst of wild flowers and the nearby river reminded Sherriff of the Itchen near Winchester. He sent home a scarlet pimpernel picked from his trench wall. It is today grey-brown and sandwiched in a fold of paper in his diary at his old school. He told his mother that if anything should happen to him, she should use his £50 savings to buy a bungalow.

The battalion trained until 9 May then marched onto Les Ciseaux and finally to some cottage billets. The march was twenty-two miles and four men collapsed. Sherriff had no idea whether they were going into the line or not. He was loath to leave the open countryside for the trenches. By mid-month the battalion entrained for Ypres and then marched to Hooge. This meant more shelling. On 17 May, Sherriff wrote home saying he was back in bed with 'the same old nagging neuralgia.' He wanted to talk to the doctor about it, but broaching the subject was hard as 'it looks as if you are shirking.' But he was also haunted by a suspicion that what lay behind his symptoms was a terrible character defect – cowardice. Neuralgia was such a feature of his life it is written into his play. Sherriff gave the condition to the officer Hibbert. Young Hibbert doesn't play rugger or cricket – a bad sign. He is apparently wealthy and keeps pornographic postcards of girls about him. He is about as unlike Sherriff as you could get. Except for his symptoms.

> Hibbert: This neuralgia of mine. I'm awfully sorry. I'm afraid
> I can't stick it any longer.

> Stanhope: No man's sent down unless he's very ill. There's
> nothing wrong with you. (Act II, 2)

In the play, Stanhope sees these headaches as scrimshanking. He loathes Hibbert and 'his repulsive little mind.' When Hibbert, who can no longer stand the fear he feels, tries to force his way past him to go down the line to see the doctor, Stanhope bars his way and tells him plainly that if he goes he will be shot in a nasty accident involving Stanhope's revolver – 'it often happens out here.'

When the threatened shot doesn't come, Hibbert lets him have the truth: 'I'm different to – to the others – you don't understand. It's got worse and worse, and now I can't bear it any longer. I'll never go up those steps again – into the line – with the men looking at me – and knowing – I'd rather die here.' Is this Sherriff recalling the humiliation of his own fear?

In the 1930 novel of *Journey's End*, co-written by Sherriff, Hibbert has a backstory that's not in the play. His mother, a widow from a proud army family, lives in penury in Cheltenham having struggled to get her son a public school education and then into the Royal Engineers. But young Hibbert has managed to put off service abroad and has avoided anything dangerous. His mother pathetically invents elaborate yarns for the benefit of the ladies in her sewing circle, of how he almost won the VC.

The play made plain Hibbert's crisis from his own mouth. 'Stanhope! I've tried like hell – I swear I have. Ever since I came out here I've hated and loathed it. Every sound up there makes me all – cold and sick.' Hibbert, persuaded by Stanhope to stay, joins in the post-operation binge after the raid on which Osborne is killed. He gets tight and boasts how he once took two tarts out for a spin in his motor after drinking too much 'port and muck' at Skindles, the Maidenhead dance venue for the in-crowd. Hibbert emerges as sleazy but he is in a way the most real and modern character in the play. Ask any drama teacher working on the text and it is Hibbert who is the one character every student instinctively understands. His fear is far more explicable than the others' courage.

In an unmade screenplay version in 1939 Sherriff had second thoughts about young Hibbert. He went over the typescript, suggesting the character be removed altogether – 'Hibbert and his troubles are not a vital part of the story.' Why on earth did he write that? Of course Hibbert is vital. He is the fly in the ointment, one of the elements that prevent the play becoming just a silly public school yarn in khaki. Sherriff blackens Hibbert in the play. Perhaps because Hibbert's is a modern mind: he will do whatever it takes to get out of the seemingly suicidal insanity of the position he and the others are in.

It would have been much easier for Sherriff to have written a rather different ending for the character and it might go something like this: Hibbert breaks down, admits to Stanhope his neuralgia is a damn lie and having faced up to his own disgrace he at last finds his courage, straightens his tie and departs the dugout with a brief word of excuse. Then he goes over the top in and walks into no-man's-land, a burst of machine gun fire signalling his end. Sherriff rightly resists any such noble cheesiness. It is the integrity of the group, the company dynamic, the play is interested in, and Hibbert stays because Stanhope lends him sufficient self-respect to face the others. Sherriff knew that king and country are on no one's mind when the shrapnel is flying. Under fire, at mud level, men will only die for their mates or an officer in whom they can find some sort of inspiration.

That is maybe one reason the play doesn't ask questions. The drama is too in the moment to take stock. Sherriff at the front wrote what he saw and what he saw was his fellow men bonded together with the superglue of shared danger. The bond was unstated, class-based and unquestioned. For Sherriff this was part of the emotional appeal of the Front – the thing that no rowing eight or rugby team or workplace could ever match. But it had a terrible price. Letting down the group whose members would be prepared to die saving him, was his greatest worry. Hibbert is unloved and untrusted by the men. Hibbert's platoon in the novel version is described as 'sullen' because his men know he'll go absent in an attack. As Sherriff piercingly wrote, 'the men with childlike simplicity, looked to their officer, their sergeant, or to one of themselves, to give them the example how to die.' The extraordinary grimness of that sentence haunts the story.

Sherriff could not entirely control his fear of shells and he was terrified of jeopardising his own men through befuddled thinking. There is something easily forgivable about his insecurity. He was also clearly a much better officer than he realised. Nobby Clark, his CO, later, when they were friends, recalled him as 'a steady unassuming young fellow of good presence. Carried a warm charm in his personality and had a certain calm, quiet air of distinction. Much respected by his men.'[12] Sherriff was too shell-battered to ever believe it. For the fictional Hibbert neuralgia was a means of escape. For Sherriff, his own very real neuralgia was the upshot of his titanic struggle to do his duty. In the play it's depicted as a transparent con. 'Neuralgia's a splendid idea. No proof, as far as I can see', says Stanhope. (Act I)

In June 1917 the battalion marched to Mic Mac Camp, on the eve of the Battle of Messines. Sherriff was organising working parties, unloading trucks and so on. He was reading *The Magnetic North*, a book by the eccentric actress Elizabeth Robins, known as 'Ibsen's High Priestess', about her experiences wandering about the Yukon. It must have made a change from the winding, trench-long sentences of Walter Scott. He turned twenty-one years old on 6 June and received an engraved matchbox from his parents. His sister Beryl sent him *The Thirty-Nine Steps*, which she recommended as 'frightfully thrilling'. From her few surviving letters Beryl sounds good value. She worked during the war as a VAD (Voluntary Aid Detachment) nurse, first in London then in Southend-on-Sea ('a dreadful place really, about as bad as Brighton!', she wrote) at the Royal Naval Hospital. She reminded him that back home they were still laughing at the same old jokes – 'one has to find something to laugh at in these times.'

His real birthday present, however, was a stay in a very modest French hotel from 9 June. By day he learnt about 'the manners & habits of the Huns' on a twelve-day sniping and intelligence course at Mont des Cats. It is the last we hear of him until July. This is because he finally got some leave or, as he calls it in a letter, ten days of 'uninterrupted happiness' in Hampton Wick. The leave was an immense relief. No shells, no neuralgia.

---

12   Michael Lucas, *The Journey's End Battalion*, p.97

Behind the lines, British troops behaved as if they were at a village fête whenever the sun came out. Sports day activities featured a three-legged race, a tug of war, tilting the bucket and sundry japes. By 22 July they were back in the trenches, C and D Companies in the front line at Klein Zillebeke. Sherriff had still to face his biggest test yet – Passchendaele, known to historians as 'Third Ypres' – the campaign of infinite misery, fought in a constant downpour in a sea of mud, that would define the war for generations to come.

Blighty One

Sherriff's war was rapidly approaching its end. In early June several hundred tons of TNT was detonated in mines beneath the Messines Ridge, the opening of Haig's plan for a mighty British push to gain the higher ground, remove the salient, and ultimately push up to the Belgian coast. The Germans were blown to pieces but the advantage was wasted in a fatal delay. With several weeks to strengthen their defences, they built a network of pillboxes with heavy machine guns. It was a low point in British strategy. It took three months and 260,000 casualties to take a local landmark, a ridge at a hamlet called Passchendaele.

Millions of shells were fired in preparation for the Passchendaele offensive which opened on 31 July with a hurricane of fire from British guns as the Fifth Army attacked on a seven mile front. Unfortunately 1917 produced the wettest summer in seventy-five years and the bombardment – four and a half million shells were fired over two weeks – only succeeded in destroying the low country's delicate drainage system. The landscape turned into a brown porridge that sucked everything into it. The suffering for men and horses was appalling.

Passchendaele gave rise to Tyne Cot, the largest of the Commonwealth War Graves Commission cemeteries. The cemetery expanded like a city and, as Geoff Dyer observed in *The Missing of the Somme*, like a city it acquired suburbs. Today, as you come in from the coach park, the sight of all those headstones in endless serried ranks is numbing. The cemetery wall has an alphabet of 34,000 inscribed names of British and Commonwealth soldiers whose remains are still lost in the mud, now an innocent gentle green slope in a rather boring bit of country.

Historians either see Passchendaele as the epitome of folly in a campaign that should have been closed down as soon as it started or as a costly strategic victory, the beginning of the end for Germany whose butcher's bill was unpayable. Until he was an old man Sherriff didn't have a view. 'I never knew a thing about the battle of Passchendaele except that I was in it. I only discovered what it was about years later when I read a history of the war.'[13] There speaks the true voice of the Poor Bloody Infantry.

On the evening of 1 August, C and D Companies of the 9/East Surrey went into the Old French Trench, two miles south-west of Ypres. Sherriff explained that he was in charge of thirty men:

> At dawn on the morning of the attack, the battalion assembled in the mud outside the huts. I lined up my platoon and went through the necessary inspection. Some of the men looked terribly ill: grey, worn faces in the dawn, unshaved and dirty because there was no clean water. I saw the characteristic shrugging of their shoulders that I knew so well. They hadn't had their clothes off for weeks, and their shirts were full of lice. Our progress to the battle area was slow and difficult. We had to move forward in single file along the duckboard tracks that were loose and slimy. If you slipped off, you went up to your knees in mud. During the walk the great bombardment from the British guns fell silent. For days it had wracked our nerves and destroyed our sleep. The sudden silence was uncanny. A sort of stagnant emptiness surrounded us. Your ears still sang from the incessant uproar, but now your mouth went dry. An orchestral overture dies away in a theatre as the curtain rises, so the great bombardment faded into silence as the infantry went into the attack. We knew now that the first wave had left the British front-line trenches, that we were soon to follow...[14]

---

13   R.C.S., *Promise of Greatness*, p.143
14   Ibid., p.145

These men were wretched, ground down by appalling food and a lack of exercise, which made the march to the assembly area particularly hard. Most of them were in their forties and out of condition. Their boots didn't fit. Many had septic blisters on their feet that needed at least a week's medical attention. Sherriff wrote, 'we had passed the point of no return.' The food was sodden biscuits and cold stew and the bacon, the troops complained, 'smelt of dead men.' Diarrhoea had broken out, men relieving themselves anywhere and everywhere. As Sherriff noted, these were the crack troops who were supposed to break through the German lines, advance to Belgium and win the war.

For the battalion it was their biggest ordeal since the Somme. Its task was to hold the captured trenches at Klein Zillebeke in the wake of the Pilckem Ridge attack. On 1 August C company moved from camp two miles south west of Ypres prior to going up to the battle front to relieve the men in the attack of the day before. Sherriff was in the second wave. They moved along slimy duckboards to the forward area. The British guns fell silent for the first time in days, an effect he compared to the dying of an orchestral overture. In front of them was a vast expanse of mud and twisted wire. It had been pelting with rain for three days solid and the Germans had dug into the gloop as best they could. The war diary states: 'C Company got caught in a heavy rain of shelling from the enemy, suffering some twenty casualties in killed and wounded. However the men were not to be discouraged and they went on cheerfully...'

Not according to Sherriff they didn't. The constant rain had soaked everyone through. The communication trenches were waist-high in toffee-coloured water. All the men could think about was getting a longed-for 'blighty one.' 'All of us, I knew, had one despairing hope in mind that we should be lucky enough to be wounded, not fatally, but severely enough to take us out of this loathsome ordeal and get us home.'[15] But the problem, he

---

15   Ibid., p.146

realiscd, was that no stretcher-bearers would ever reach anyone in the impossible mud.

The order came to climb out of the trenches. The rotten sandbags fell apart as they heaved themselves over. The shelling had been so heavy there was not a landmark left. They might as well have been on the moon. Sherriff and his men tripped on submerged barbed wire, which ripped their legs. The mud was blown everywhere by 'coalboxes', shells that exploded in a cloud of black smoke. Decaying bodies from previous fighting were occasionally blown up into the humid air and the stench was appalling. The first wave of East Surreys was wiped out by machine gun fire and had rolled into waterlogged craters where they floated like wax dolls.

Sherriff arrived at the shattered German trench to find it full of wounded and dying British soldiers. The improvised first aid station was useless as the doctor and his orderlies were all dead. The engineers whose job it was to lay telegraph wires had also been killed so Morse communication was impossible. The remnants of the first wave – 15 out of 100 men – were cut off. All he could do was give first aid. Sherriff went to work, applying pathetically inadequate bandages to huge gaping wounds, comforting the men. His work in that trench with the dying that afternoon was heroic although he describes it as 'only a matter of watching them slowly bleed to death'. But it is reasonable to think that he found the inner strength he had always craved, able to carry on under fire, his fear banished, reassuring the dying as one by one they slipped away. He had once talked in his letters of how much he would prefer to treat wounds than to cause them. Now he got his chance and he proved himself a superb officer, doing what he could with calm compassion.

At some point he and a runner were ordered by Warre-Dymond to find B Company. He made his way down shattered trenches. A whizz-bang glanced the top of a pillbox five yards from him. Sherriff thought at first his whole face had been blown away. Plastered in mud and blood but still conscious, he was sent back on foot to find a dressing station. 'The doctor swabbed our wounds on our hands and faces and tried to see through the holes in our uniforms where pieces of debris had gone in. 'You don't seem to have got anything very deep. Can you go on?' The trip took forever as he staggered across the mud. At the base hospital, a doctor removed fifty-two pieces of pea-sized concrete from Sherriff's face, right hand and torso. 'One for every week of the year... I needed no souvenir to remind me of the monstrous disgrace of Passchendaele.' [16]

The 10th Casualty Clearing Station at Abeele received over 2000 casualties on the first two days of the offensive, including a hundred Germans. Sherriff is mentioned as wounded in the war diary for 2 August as is his friend Percy High. That day he wrote to his mother a letter that, because of his injured hand, looks as if it was by a nine-year-old.

Dear Mother

I am writing to say that I am feeing quite well although I was wounded this morning in the right hand and in the right side of the face. Nothing at all serious Dear, don't worry, I walked down alright... I am very lucky, I think to get off so lightly, considering what some of my men got... I will write you further (unless I have got a "blighty") and tell you more about it.

But rest content that I am quite well: there is a chance of getting home.

I have a job to write as my hand is like my face, peppered all over with little bits.

From your loving son, Bob. [17]

To his father he wrote on 8 August:

---

16   Ibid., p.149-150
17   2 August 1917

Dear Pips

Am writing this left-handed as my right is *hors de combat* at present. I was hit by several small splinters also on the right side of my face – the shell was so close that the big pieces went over my head – it burst about 5 feet away; lucky for me my wounds are none worse and the shell no bigger.

I feel quite fit no pain – hope to get to England.

Am very much bound up and look worse than I feel.

Hoping to see you soon.

From your loving son

Bob

He was very lucky to be alive. His comrade Lieutenant William Sadler – possibly caught in the same shell burst as Sherriff – died of his wounds the next day. Sadler's fate has been researched by Van Emden and Piuk in their book *Famous: 1914-1918*. Hopefully thinking there might have been a muddle, Sadler's distraught father wrote to the War Office for clarification of his boy's death and asked that the reply be sent to a neighbour's flat to spare his wife the sight of another telegram. She was already ill with worry about their other son also fighting in France. The bad news was duly confirmed. It took Mr Sadler a week to pluck up the courage to tell his wife. Families in Britain and Germany were swamped with a huge wave of grief as casualty rates ballooned in early August.

Three days after his exit from the front Sherriff's battalion was massively shelled, the rain sheeted down and the mud jammed their guns. A German raiding party attacked under cover of a mist. The battalion took 151 casualties in the first week of August. Among them was Colonel Henry de la Fontaine. A sniper caught him recce-ing the Germans' position. He was in his mid-forties and had been with the regiment since he was nineteen. He made it his business to know every man in the battalion by name and regarded them, in his civilised phrase, as 'their superior in rank but their equal in humanity.' 'A personal friend of, and beloved by, every man in the Battalion, he died for the safety of his men', records the battalion war diary with rare emotion. The colonel would take his place in Sherriff's roll of honour in his diary.

Sherriff was soon back in England, convalescing at the British Red Cross Hospital at Netley, near Southampton. His wounds were not too bad but he was lucky not to have been blinded. He was also perhaps lucky to have been sent home: his was a borderline blighty. His friend Lindsay wrote to him about the new commander Le Fleming ('a ripping chap – you'd like him') and was breezily snobbish about the new officer intake. 'My dear boy, we have 11 new subalterns.... They have hardly an aitch between them and are very terrible people I can't stick at any price.'[18] Sherriff wrote to his friend Webb (congratulating him on his MC) about not being able to wait to get back to 'the dear old 9th'. But he wrote to his father on 18 August: 'I shall not of course hesitate to report any trouble with my head for I think 10½ months is quite a sufficient spell out there and that I am due at least a couple of months off in England.'

Sherriff also wrote home saying that he was uncomfortable about exaggerating his neuralgia symptoms to the Medical Board which was minded to grant him three weeks leave and three weeks home service at the barracks at Dover (with the 3/ East Surrey) before returning him to the Front. Sherriff never had to go back to France. He stayed with the Home Service from November 1917 to January 1919 acting as musketry officer and gas officer when he was promoted to lieutenant and then finally de-mobbed in January 1919 with the rank of Captain, having been stationed in Glasgow.

He had survived the worst conflict in human history and the relief must have been overwhelming. He was not a natural officer. When he was famous, at a battalion reunion dinner he made a speech and asked a question of his commanding officer, Nobby Clark: 'I wonder if you remember, Sir, what you said

18   Letter to R.C.S., 20 September 1917

to me when I reported to you that I had just been wounded and that I was to be evacuated? "Afraid I don't," said Nobby. You said, "Thank God," remarked Sherriff, and sat down to soldierly applause.' [19]

When Sherriff came to writing the play he set it in the run-up to Thursday, 21 March 1918 (the play's action closes on the dawn of that day), a date that means nothing much now. But to the audiences of *Journey's End* in 1929 it was hugely significant. A pivotal day and 'the most dangerous moment of the war for the Allied cause.'[20] The German objective was one massive all-out effort to 'beat the British' still undefeated on the Western Front. The plan was to launch a war-winning assault before the slow build-up of American troops in France could make a difference. The Russians had accepted crushing peace terms earlier in the month, freeing up vast numbers of German troops for a big push at St Quentin where the play is set. It was known as Operation Michael or *Kaiserschlacht* (the Kaiser's Battle). The German order was given: 'The Michael attack will take place on March 21. Break the first enemy positions at 9.40am.' That is just a few hours after the play ends: the curtain comes down on the sound of the first shells of an almighty dawn barrage known as 'Bruchmüller's Symphony' after the artillery officer who conducted it. Over a million shells were fired in five hours on a sixty-mile front. The British troops curled into a collective foetal ball and endured it.

Casualty rates in the coming days were among the highest of the war. The German advance – using fast moving units of storm troopers bypassing points of resistance – was hugely successful and gained thirty-eight miles, causing mayhem. It was so devastating that on 11 April Haig gave his famous 'backs to the wall' order in which he said: 'each one of us must fight to the end…every position must be held to the last man.' The British Fifth Army heroically contested every single yard. The German

19   Rosa Maria Bracco, *Merchants of Hope*, p.170
20   Andrew Roberts, *A History of the English-Speaking Peoples Since 1900*, p.136

advance would over-reach itself. It eventually petered out and was finally reversed at enormous cost to both sides.

Ten years later Britons were all too aware of what an epic ordeal that March Retreat had been. The British survivors of that barrage used the same phrase – 'all hell let loose'. They experienced a near-constant earthquake. Gregory Clarke's sound effects at the close of play in *Journey's End* were so loud it hurt: the whistling and explosions were unbelievable. Even so, it was just the merest hint of what it must have been like in reality.

So what happened to Sherriff's beloved battalion? The previous few days it had been in reserve. On 21 March they were holding a position at Villecholles. Lieutenant Colonel Le Fleming (De La Fontaine's replacement) was caught in the open on a recce and shot dead. Laurence Le Fleming's loss was another bad blow. At thirty-eight he was not only an excellent CO but also an acclaimed cricketer who had played for Kent. His well-known brother, John, who survived the war, was a former rugby international and schoolmaster and their father was a vicar. In Sherriff's eyes both the Le Fleming brothers had the dream CV. Yet, oddly, the Colonel he was to create in *Journey's End* could not have been more different. He is unable to remonstrate with his superiors on behalf of the men's safety and he is forgetful of the human cost of the raid he has supervised. When he orders the German prisoner's pockets to be turned out (which contain, schoolboy style, a bit of string, fruit drops and a pen knife) you get the impression of a not very inspiring head boy in front of a first-year. Sherriff for some reason divorced the best COs he knew from the one he sketched in his play.

On 23 March the 9/East Surrey had to retreat across the Somme from Falvy to Pargny. D Company had to swim for it, the enemy pressing in all the time and by the end of the day the battalion had taken heavy losses against crack German troops. The crisis came on 26 March when the 9/East Surrey found itself occupying the old German line east of Rosières. The battalion was reduced by a fierce attack to about 300 men holding 1,000 yards of mostly open ground. They were soon completely surrounded after an aborted withdrawal. The decision to jump into an old communication trench and fight it out was taken by the replacement commander Nobby Clark (he had originally assigned Sherriff to C Company) who despite being savagely wounded in the face by a shell was carrying on. To the men he was a figure of huge respect and amiability. Nobby gave it to them straight: 'You will either be killed or captured before the morning is out. Stick it out for the honour of the Regiment.'

That's precisely what they did. The regimental history records 'a great number of acts of heroism' against heavy odds in this amazing last stand by the battalion. Two unnamed Lewis gunners kept firing until their gun was destroyed by a bomb blast. Badly injured the pair picked up their rifles and continued firing until they were both killed. Lance Corporal Bradley continued to work his Lewis gun alone despite being shot through the chest. Lieutenant Grant kept up a lethal fire until he was shot through the head. The Germans kept coming and were repeatedly beaten back, their dead thickly strewn around. Eventually the thin khaki line was down to its last round and the Germans were finally able to rush them. There were just two unwounded officers and fifty-five men left when they were taken prisoner. Captain Warre-Dymond would win the MC for his galvanizing leadership and obliviousness to danger while under relentless mortar and machine gun fire. Michael Lucas in his history of the battalion quotes Fred Billman, who was badly wounded and wrote to his wife with classic Tommy understatement: 'Well darling, I guess you are wondering why you have not heard from me, but it's been a bit busy over here lately.'[21] A bit busy!

In the film *This Happy Breed* set between the wars in south London, Noël Coward includes a toast to the East Surrey, the regiment Coward might have joined. The 9th was by then famous. When Sherriff came to write up his diary, he included in the dedication some names.

---

21 Lucas, *The Journey's End Battalion*, p.139

In writing these pages I have always in mind the memory of:

Lieut. Colonel H T M de la Fontaine DSO
Major Anderson VC
Captain Lindsay MC
Lieut. Douglass
Lieut. Patterson
2nd Lieut. Millard
2nd Lieut. Trench
2nd Lieut. Kiber
Lieut. Picton
Lieut. Grant
Captain Pirie
Lieut. Sadler

who were all killed, fighting with the 9th East Surreys in the Ypres Salient, on Vimy Ridge, in the Valley of the Somme and on the plains around Loos.

These were much the same men who would one day walk into his play complaining about no pepper.

Riverbank Amdram

When Sherriff got home he went back to work as if nothing had happened. His wounds soon healed and he went back to work as an 'outdoorman' for the Sun, on a beat between Putney and Windsor, inspecting properties for flood and fire risk.

We would, perhaps, never have heard of Sherriff had it not been for a leaky rowing eight. In 1921 Kingston Rowing Club, of which he was a keen member, needed £100 for a new boat. As secretary of the entertainments subcommittee, Sherriff was detailed to come up with a show that might serve as a fundraiser. Unable to find a suitable play for a cast of burly rowers, he sat down and wrote a skit that involved a coachload of trippers going on an outing to Brighton. *A Hitch in the Proceedings*, staged in November 1921, was a one-act farce. Sherriff played the Rev. Teddington Locke with his brother Bundy as the bus driver. It was a huge success, largely because two teachers from his old school played a pair of red-nosed drunks and the schoolboys in the audience, expecting to be bored, laughed themselves sick.

The money was raised and Sherriff got his first taste of writing for the stage. The 'smoker' set a pattern for several further plays, all by Sherriff. It was decided he was the club's natural scribe. He bought a copy of *Play-Making* by William Archer and read it very thoroughly. The Kingston Adventurers Dramatic Society initially performed at The Gables, a 250-seat mini-theatre in Surbiton, built in 1882 by the matchstick millionaire Wilberforce Bryant. In 1900 the theatre was converted to a private military hospital for the wounded of the Boer War. It later reverted to theatre use and Sherriff and his rowers used it prior to it becoming, in 1927, the Hillcroft Theatre long since demolished. The Gables was where Sherriff's career began with a series of inoffensive playlets.

The Woods of Meadowside followed, in April 1922, in which Mrs Pepper is anxious to improve the fortunes of her daughter by marrying money. A picnic is arranged; the parson arrives (Sherriff playing another silly ass vicar) as does the Countess of Surbiton and three racecourse thieves in disguise. Beryl Sherriff played Mrs Trayler-Gush. It went down well and to the approval of the critic of the *Surrey Comet*.

Sherriff sent the manuscript to literary agents Curtis Brown (he picked them, he recalled, as the name sounded unpretentious) who politely declined it, as they did *Profit and Loss*, a three-act comedy set in Mayfair between 1913-1919, about a building foreman who makes a fortune making entrenching tools during the war and gets a knighthood. The one note of seriousness is the play's implicit disapproval of wartime profiteers. The show was another nod to the plays of J. M. Barrie – featuring class reversals, home truths and a butler – and was well received.

His next piece *Cornlow-in-the-Downs*, around 1924, was about a village in Sussex where the inhabitants talk of apricots, croquet, fishing, but never money. It is a story of a village tradition versus modernization and it featured Beryl Sherriff but not Robert. Curtis Brown, modestly impressed, this time gave it to Sunday repertory companies to read. Nothing came of it.

His next play was *The Feudal System*, in 1925. Three acts with French windows. In it a butler brings up a wastrel's heir after the wastrel shoots himself and a frightful vulgarian buys up the estate. The butler through canny land speculation makes enough money to buy back the estate and to carry on working for the lad he has raised as his own. The loyal servant has the line 'England is full of worms who'd like to see the grand old houses and the grand old families go under.'

Mr Bridie's Finger would be the last of his five plays for the club. Reading those unpublished playscripts, it is frankly not easy to spot a writer who would one day make it as a West End dramatist. But the experience of acting in his own work must have been invaluable. He was simply waiting for the right subject, something he could pour himself into, to come along.

The background to all this drama was the Thames. Sherriff's captaincy of the Kingston Rowing Club was very successful. For five years he rowed at Henley in the Thames Cup eights and he was in the crew that broke the course record time in 1926. He remained exceptionally fit and was both a superb oarsman and coach. Years later, he went to Oxford as a mature student and rowed in the New College eight in a crew half his age; it was only a bout of pleurisy that prevented him getting a Blue. In *The Dam Busters*, his last film, the camera lingers on the river trophies above the door of a missing crew member's quarters – a detail that is perhaps Sherriff's discreet signature.

But by the time Sherriff came to write *Journey's End* he was no longer Captain of Boats, he was writing in the evenings for his own amusement. By 1927, he turned to a novel he had started and put in the bottom drawer. It was, initially, a story of hero worship in which Stanhope, the school prefect, is ruined by all the adoration of the younger boys. Drifting from job to job after school, he is then helped by the successful Raleigh who had been a mug at games but was inspired by his hero. Sherriff couldn't make the thing work. He introduced the war as a backdrop and put Raleigh in the same trench as Stanhope, distilling the school yarn into a few days on the Front and confining the action entirely to the trench – the five key characters drawn from life. The act of writing it was a nostalgic return to the front and the play was open house for the men of C Company. 'I was writing about something real, about men I had lived with and knew so well that every line they spoke came straight from them and not from me.'[22]

He started the play in early 1927 and – having wondered whether to call it *Suspense* or *Waiting* – hit upon the title when he read in a book (he could later not recall the title) the closing sentence of a chapter: 'It was late in the evening when we came at last to our Journey's End.' He sent it to Curtis Brown in the April of 1928. They replied saying they thought it a 'very fine play'

---

22 R.C.S., *No Leading Lady*, p.37

adding 'whether we can interest a management remains to be seen.'

A meeting was quickly arranged with Geoffrey Dearmer, on the committee of the Incorporated Stage Society, the most likely of the private theatre 'Sunday clubs' to stage such an uncommercial piece. (Dearmer was the last of the Great War poets to die at the age of 103 in 1996.) Sherriff regarded the society as suspiciously highbrow. But he visited Dearmer while his play *Paul Among the Jews* was on. Dearmer loved *Journey's End* but the committee was divided. It advised Sherriff to get a sponsor to secure the votes needed for a green light.

There was only one man whose opinion would ensure the production – Bernard Shaw, whose word was then holy writ. Shaw at the time was floating off Cap d'Antibes in a rubber ring. Sherriff sent him his play. Shaw read it and wrote back (returning the stamps Sherriff had enclosed) a report:

> The play is, properly speaking, a document, not a drama. The war produced several of them. They require a good descriptive reporter, with a knack of dialogue. They are accounts of catastrophes, and sketches of trench life, useful as correctives to the romantic conception of war; and they are usually good of their kind because those who cannot do them well do not do them at all.
>
> They seem to me useless as dramatists' credentials. The best of them cannot prove that the writer could produce a comedy or tragedy with ordinary materials. Having read this *Journey's End*, and found it as interesting as any other vivid description of a horrible experience, I could give the author a testimonial as a journalist; but I am completely in the dark as before concerning his qualification for the ordinary professional work of a playwright, which does not admit of burning the house to roast the pig.
>
> As a 'slice of life' – horrible abnormal life – I should say let it be performed by all means, even at the disadvantage of being

the newspaper of the day before yesterday. But if I am asked to express an opinion as to whether the author could make a living as a playwright, I can only say I don't know. I can neither encourage nor discourage him.[23]

G Bernard Shaw

It's a curiously obtuse reading of the play and one wonders whether he read it in a rush. Sherriff cannily reported back to the committee the 'let it be performed by all means' bit and left out the rest. The show was opted for by a single vote margin. That, anyway, was Sherriff's version of events.

Matthew Norgate, however, who was secretary of the Stage Society, years later shared a secret with the readers of his weekly gossip column.[24] According to him, the society had been utterly desperate for a show to fill their December slot. It had made up its mind to stage the play regardless of Shaw's opinion. Norgate said he had asked pacifist dramatist and war veteran Miles Malleson – to become the well-known Ealing Studios character actor with the pointy nose and double chin – to direct Journey's End for the fee of fifteen guineas. Malleson declined. It was a decision, Norgate gleefully told his readers, that cost him a fortune.

The job went to the untried James Whale, the son of a Black Country furnaceman, who had served on the front and was now a jobbing actor doing time in Noel Pemberton-Billing's play High Treason. He had made his stage debut in 1922, had worked with John Gielgud and a coterie of promising young actors, and was keen to direct. Whale was also a gifted artist, having absorbed the designs he saw on his many student visits to the Dudley Opera House.

In his flat in Chelsea he built a beautiful model for the dugout, to become the most famous set of its era. Sherriff had vaguely imagined a simple cavern. Whale had created a dugout in which the timbers pressed down onto the actors, an underground crucible for the life of the men on the front. It was

23   Letter to R.C.S., 16 September 1928
24   *Variety News*, 12 March 1936

perfect. It exuded frontline squalor, candlelight and something else. He had given it, Sherriff wrote, 'a touch of crude romance that was fascinating and exhilarating. Above all, it was real. There may never have been a dugout like this one: but any man who had lived in the trenches would say, "This is it: this is what it was like". '[25]

The show was deliberately cast with no star names because they couldn't afford any. Whale wanted the play to stand out, not the actors. He offered the lead to the twenty-one-year-old Laurence Olivier who had just finished in John Drinkwater's *Bird in Hand* at the Royalty Theatre. For the ultra-ambitious, engaged-to-be-married Olivier, *Journey's End* was just a stopgap. He took the part on condition that Whale got the director Basil Dean to attend the show. Dean – whose casts were famously drilled like soldiers and woe betide any slackers – had contracted him as a leading man in his forthcoming big budget version of the desert classic *Beau Geste*. Olivier was desperate to leave the trenches and join the more glamorous Foreign Legion in the West End where his moustache would be better noticed.

The first *Journey's End* production would get just two performances (9 and 10 December 1928), a Sunday evening and a Monday matinee, at the Apollo Theatre on Shaftesbury Avenue. In freezing rehearsal rooms above Charing Cross Road Olivier looked bored and restless at the read-through. Sherriff had his day job to do, so he missed most of the rehearsals. The actor who had been hired to play Mason the cook walked into the room and tossed the script on the table, announcing he had got another part for a longer run and promptly left. At the first reading, recalled Sherriff: 'The men huddled around the table hunched in their overcoats: some with mufflers around their necks. Some with their hats on – as unlike war strained soldiers in a front-line dugout as they could possibly be. They sat with their eyes glued to their scripts, puffing cigarettes, never making an attempt to emphasise or dramatise their lines; but as the reading went on it came over beyond a shadow of a doubt

25 R.C.S., *No Leading Lady* p.48

that the team had been perfectly chosen. None had any need to act the parts – they *were* the men – they merely had to be themselves.[26]

The cuts to the script were negligible and the cast was confirmed:

Captain Hardy	David Horne
Lieutenant Osborne	George Zucco
Private Mason	Alexander Field
Second Lieutenant Raleigh	Maurice Evans
Captain Stanhope	Laurence Olivier
Second Lieutenant Trotter	Melville Cooper
Second Lieutenant Hibbert	Robert Speaight
Company Sergeant-Major	Percy Walsh
The Colonel	H. G. Stoker
German soldier	Geoffrey Wincott

There was little money for costumes so Sherriff lent Olivier his old Sam Browne belt, revolver and his captain's tunic, which only needed Stanhope's MC ribbon sewing on. The part was thus physically handed on from author to actor. Olivier's performance as Stanhope was possibly designed to show what he might have been like in uniform at the front had he been old enough to join up. Whatever, he was brilliantly cast, effortlessly bringing to the role the soldierly glamour, the melancholy, and an explosive ferocity of temper.

The race to get the show on a Sunday performance after two weeks rehearsal was frenetic. As the audience filed in, Sherriff was in a muck sweat. Whale went backstage. Basil Dean turned up with Madeleine Carroll, one of Hitchcock's future blondes, on his arm. The verdict was that it was honest and good but hopelessly uncommercial. Barry Jackson and other managers turned up but their feeling was that although everyone liked the play they all thought no one else would. Monday's matinee performance would, however, be the crucial test as that was the

---

26   Ibid., p.52

show attended by society members and critics who didn't want to go out on a Sunday night.

Olivier had been sensational as Stanhope. But he only ever gave three performances (the third was a charity performance in the 1930s), a fact he was to regret for the rest of his life. One key point about *Journey's End* is that its West End success didn't just happen. It was the result of determined campaigning by theatre critics: they spotted it, nurtured it and closed protective ranks around what they saw as a very special piece of work. Their support was almost messianic. Key reactions to it came from the *Daily Express*'s Hannen Swaffer who liked to refer to himself as the paper's 'Editorial Insultant'. Through syndication 'Swaff' claimed 20 million readers. He was often so drunk on first nights that managements frequently tried to shut him out, causing appalling scenes in foyers. He declared *Journey's End* 'The Greatest Of All War Plays'. 'There is no shirking the facts, no concession to fashion. It is perfectly acted, each actor cuts a little cameo of stark reality. All London should flock to see it.'

James Agate was, however, the show's most powerful advocate. He wrote prolifically about plays for *The Sunday Times* and also broadcast regularly as the BBC's theatre critic. A Lancashire man, he famously sported the checked garb of a bookmaker. He had served with the Army Service Corps and had even written the army handbook on hay procurement. His readers certainly did not know that when reviewing in Paris he frequented the male brothel recommended by Marcel Proust. Agate was walking past the Apollo after his customary long lunch. He bumped into the freelance critic George Bishop and asked what was being played. Bishop told him to get into the theatre smartish for the second act. Agate did. After the show, he raced to the BBC, tore up his intended script and wrote another on *Journey's End* and delivered his sermon. 'I cannot believe that there was any single member of the audience this afternoon who was not only deeply moved but also exalted and even exhilarated by this tragedy...' he spoke in what was the most important press reaction to the play, even though he had only seen half of it. It was outrageous that work of this quality could vanish after two performances, he said. He lambasted cowardly managements 'adamant in their belief that war plays have no audience in the theatre.' He also weighed into the depressing conservatism of London theatregoers. 'The wrong lies entirely with the public which will not support good plays and has a taste only for the bare knees of musical comedy. It is the public's fault if it is deprived of work of extraordinary quality and interest which brings one into touch with the greatest experience known to living man.'[27]

Agate threw down a gauntlet to a producer to step forth and take on a show that had no leading lady or pretty sets. Commercial managements were wary of glowing reviews and regarded the Stage Society as a home of lost causes and lost critics. It's at this point in the story that the penniless and importunate Maurice Browne entered the scene – wearing gold earrings. The son of a cleric, Browne was educated at Winchester and Cambridge and regarded himself as an actor-poet with an agenda against the hidebound flapper-happy theatre of his day. Intensely idealistic, he wanted to start what he rather tweely called in his memoirs 'a cloud theatre'. In Florence he had met and proposed to Ellen van Volkenburg, known as 'Nellie Van', an amateur actress and the daughter of a well-off Chicago meat salesman. Browne pawned the family silver and followed her to Chicago where in 1912 they set up their 'Little Theatre' on the fourth floor of the famous Fine Arts Building. This 100-seat venue was committed to the production of non-commercial drama, partly inspired by the Abbey Players from Dublin who visited the city in 1911 with *The Playboy of the Western World*.

Browne was extremely pernickety about his productions. Programmes were printed on special Japanese paper so they didn't rustle and latecomers were ruthlessly barred. The emphasis was on imaginative, highly conceptual presentations on tiny budgets. Their repertoire included work by Shaw, Strindberg, Schnitzler, Yeats and others. But *The Trojan Woman* by Euripides

27   James Agate, *My Theatre Talks*, p.135

(in Gilbert Murray's translation) was their signature production and, the first time the play had been seen in the United States. Chicagoans watched Hecuba surveying a ruined Troy, which after years of siege has been taken and sacked by the Greeks. Her husband and son are killed, her daughter raped and her people enslaved. All she has left is her little grandson. The Greeks, fearing the boy will become a rallying point for Trojan resistance, throw him from the walls of the city.

An indictment of all wars then and since, Browne billed it as 'The World's Greatest Peace Play' and toured the production throughout the mid-west with Nellie Van gnashing and wailing as Hecuba. The tour was partly funded by the Women's Peace Party as a propaganda tool. It lost heavily. But the 'Little Theatre' format caught fire. Within five years there were thirty such theatres in a fifty-mile radius of New York's Times Square and over a thousand nationwide by the end of the 1920s. The key companies in the movement turned fully professional. Browne was thus the British father of the movement in America. He spent the post-war years looking for a Euripidean peace play without swords or sandals.

In 1928, he was back in London having some success as an actor, starring as a French soldier in Paul Raynal's symbolical war tragedy *The Unknown Warrior* (*Le tombeau sous l'Arc de Triomphe*) in an English version by the writer and pilot Cecil Lewis who had shot down several enemy planes over the Somme in his Sopwith Camel. (His book, *Sagittarius Rising*, would become a secondary source for *Aces High*, the 1976 airborne film version of *Journey's End* scripted by Howard Barker.) Browne became a bit of a celebrity even though it was widely acknowledged in the business that he was a rotten actor. *The Unknown Warrior* was highly regarded, though almost no one went to see it. Shaw said, 'it was worth having a war to get such a play as this'[28] – a remark which over-rated the play and under-rated the war.

Browne had two very powerful friends in the Elmhirsts. An American, Dorothy Elmhirst (née Whitney) was one of the richest women in the world having inherited several fortunes.

28 Michael Young, *The Elmhirsts of Dartington*, p.218

Widowed in the great influenza epidemic, she married Leonard Elmhirst, an Englishman from an old Yorkshire family. In 1925 the couple bought Dartington Hall in Devon, which they made famous as a pioneering place of agricultural and artistic experiment. They were keen to bring on new writing for the theatre and prepared to stump up the money for it. Browne staged *The Unknown Warrior* for them at Dartington and the exhausted couple duly promised to back Browne's next project with the advice 'wait until you find a play you *have* to do.' They gave him a £400 cash advance.

Browne only had to wait ten days. It was his friend the poet Harold Monro who saw *Journey's End* at the evening performance and at two in the morning, doubtless worse for wear, rang Browne to tell him it was 'thrillingly wonderful.' He called again in the morning to gush some more. His ecstatic opinion was confirmed by leading actors at the Arts Theatre Club who had been along to see it en masse. George Bishop knew Browne a bit and thought the show might do nicely for his first stab at management and scoured London looking for him. Browne called up Sherriff's agents and asked for a script.

Sherriff's alarm bells went off when he had heard that Browne was, as he put in his autobiography, 'an intellectual dedicated to the production of highbrow plays to uplift the theatre and pay homage to art for art's sake' as if that were some dreadful crime. But he went over to Browne's empty flat and left the script for him. Browne went straight down to Dartington by train and read it aloud to the Elmhirsts who were deeply and sincerely moved, Leonard having lost two brothers in the war.

When Browne and Sherriff met, the latter was surprised to find negotiations were already underway to book the Savoy Theatre in the Strand where the long run of John Van Druten's previously banned *Young Woodley* (a shocking drama in which a seventeen-year-old public schoolboy kisses his housemaster's wife) was shortly to end. The ball was by now rolling fast. Agate made a second BBC broadcast applauding Browne's plans for the play but he predicted abject failure for any attempt to raise the tone of the West End: 'It is utterly, totally and completely impossible for him or anybody else to make a theatre pay in this country which is not devoted to musical comedy or imbecile farce.'[29] It was his challenge to both managements and the public. In those days, critics were fabulously rude to their readers.

Browne was determined to have a go with the Elmhirst money. He, Sherriff and Whale were decided that the cast should remain the same for the West End transfer. Olivier, however, would have to be replaced as he had been signed up for *Beau Geste*. The others were free. Browne had plans to play Osborne himself but mercifully he gave way and George Zucco got his part back. The next task was to find a replacement for Olivier as Stanhope. Colin Clive was suggested by his actress fiancée. Browne went to see him playing Steve in *Show Boat* and liked the look of him. The actor had the perfect background. His father was Colonel C. P. Colin Clive-Greig and the family was descended from Robert Clive (1725-1774) known as Clive of India. Colin had been educated at Stonyhurst College and Sandhurst before abandoning the army career he had set his heart on due to a bad knee injury. Instead of going into the cavalry he joined Hull Repertory Company.

Clive was a complicated, neurotic person but of an essentially sweet nature. He was gay, hopelessly alcoholic, and awkwardly attached to Jeanne de Casalis, a French playwright/actress who kept having affairs with other women. (She would become a friend of Sherriff's and together they wrote *St Helena*, which was staged on Broadway in 1936 with Maurice Evans playing Napoleon.) Clive launched his career with the performance. It led him directly to Hollywood where he teamed up with Whale on the 1931 film *Frankenstein* in which the monster stomps about a blasted landscape curiously reminiscent of the Somme.

Today the boring doctrine is that acting and alcohol never mix, that there's no such thing as a great performance given under the influence. If true, Clive was the exception that proved the rule. At the read-through he stammered and fluffed his lines.

29   Ibid., p.135

At lunch he went to the pub and came back a new man. 'The whisky at lunch had freed him from his inhibitions, and the words flowed without restraint,[30] said Sherriff. The probable truth is that Clive never once gave an even faintly sober performance. But he was magnificent all the same. What he did was to reveal a portrait of a young who had lost his soul to the war.

If the film version is anything to go by, he was especially wonderful at the character's seething paranoia, the words tumbling out through a fog of booze: 'You know he'll write and tell her I reek of whisky all day… I'm captain of this company. What's that bloody little prig of a boy matter? D'you see? He's a little prig.' His was a gloriously over-the-top portrait of a soldier used to going over the top.

The story of how Clive got the part of Stanhope varies depending on who is telling it. Sherriff recalled that Browne didn't want Clive at all and preferred Colin Keith-Johnston, a handsome actor who had been in *Prisoners of War* with Whale and Raymond Massey. Moreover he was an ex-officer who had played Stanhope for real in the trenches, winning the MC. He didn't get the part. It was the young Maurice Evans – as Raleigh – who argued for Clive's more inspirational audition and won Browne and Sherriff over. On New Year's Day it was announced the play would be presented on 21 January 1929 at the Savoy. Soon the slogan 'All Roads Lead to *Journey's End*' was on every other omnibus in London.

At the Apollo the sound of machine gunfire was a cane being repeatedly thrashed onto a chair cushion. Shells were thunder-flash bombs chucked into a steel tank. The acoustics were massively improved at the Savoy, though getting the volumes right was near impossible. Rehearsals went on until midnight the night before the show opened. A lighting and effects rehearsal was called for ten in the morning and a dress rehearsal that afternoon. On opening night Sherriff was advised to go backstage and see the troops – except for Clive who was no doubt staring into a glass darkly in his dressing room. As the

30 R.C.S., *No Leading Lady*, p.78

audience arrived, Sherriff went into a box to watch the show that would change his life forever.

The newspapers reported on the first night a sprinkling of military top brass including Sir Noel Birch, director of artillery, Lord Kitchener's private secretary, General Alfred Critchley (made a general at the age of twenty-seven) and General Plumer. The Elmhirsts were there and many fashionable stage writers – John Drinkwater, John Van Druten, Edward Knoblock, and St. John Ervine. Mrs Sherriff sensibly took egg sandwiches and a flask of whisky and soda. The cast was on flying form. Clive was superb and the bombs went off in all the right places.

Sherriff assumed naively that the audience was bored throughout. When the curtain fell at the Savoy, the audience remained utterly silent. The curtain went up on the actors and the curtain went down again. Still nothing. Then out of the darkness a punter broke ranks and emitted a solitary 'Bravo!' The audience started to clap and the audience kicked into life. By the time Evans, Zucco and, finally, Clive came on the applause was deafening – 'like a hail storm on a roof barn.' It was thunderous, sustained approval. One paper reported that even the critics cheered – most unlikely if today's critics are anything to go by.

The papers were beside themselves. 'It could and should be translated into the language of every ex-ally and ex-enemy,' said *The Chronicle*. 'This noble war play,' said the *Morning Post*. 'Great war drama' said Alan Parsons in the *Daily Mail*. The praise was in the headlines and the copy of most of the reviews consisted of plot description, a bit of gush, then a paragraph listing the actors. *The Times'* unsigned notice was almost certainly written by Charles Morgan, a war veteran who had seen action at the defence of Antwerp. He had previously referred to Olivier as 'a fiery particle' in a cast 'who drew the audience into communion with their suffering and their concealments of it.' He set the pattern of all the reviews at the Savoy by applauding the play's realism. 'How like it all is!' he nostalgically started the review, seeing the play as 'a series of scenes almost as unrelated and as difficult of interpretation as they would be in actual life.'[31]

Richard Jennings in *The Spectator* magazine wrote about the audience. While Sherriff's play was painful it was not as painful he wrote, 'as the behaviour of the rowdies who clattered in, late at the beginning, late after every interval – rows of fatuous women clanking their hideous pearls and beads, munching chocolates, smoking without permission, and clamouring for programmes from their sheepish men.'[32] He ended up wishing the play a long run and hoping that its audiences didn't turn it into a farce.

The *Evening Standard* announced 'Young Playwright's Great Triumph' – a huge help at the box office. By the afternoon a queue had formed around the Savoy. Hotels were demanding rows of expensive seats. The show was turning into a major draw. The ticket agencies were crucial and in this case they offered Browne a four-week deal guaranteeing a nightly block of seats. Browne held out for a twelve-week deal and stuck to it. The agency reps walked out in fury as negotiations broke down. Sherriff tried to fathom why Browne was taking such a risk with his baby. For the eccentric Browne, it was no doubt his sweet and belated revenge on the commercial theatre to which his whole life was opposed. He had them over a barrel. Sherriff pretended it wasn't happening and went back to his insurance rounds.

In the event Maurice Browne was brilliant. He kept his nerve and pulled off the biggest deal ever for a straight play in the West End: a three-month guarantee of a £1,000 a week. Spencer Curtis Brown, who represented Sherriff and had cautiously encouraged him from the start of his career, negotiated an unusual agreement that if the receipts were to go over £1,500 a week he would get ten per cent throughout, which soon meant £250 per week (a huge sum and over thirty times his Sun salary). He had effectively won the lottery – and this was before the global franchise the play would soon become. Sherriff's friends from the Sun had been there on the first night as the rowing club crowd. The chief

31 *The Times*, 22 January 1929
32 *The Spectator*, 29 January 1929

clerk of Sherriff's firm rang to congratulate him and assumed he would be leaving his job now he had such a smash hit on his hands. Sherriff was horrified. He had no concept of being a professional writer. What if his next play should flop? The theatre was a fickle mistress, he reasoned. He was eventually persuaded to leave by the Sun's chairman with the assurance his job would be kept open for at least a year.

The show backstage at the Savoy was soon being run like the royal yacht. Stagehands wore white trousers, Maurice Browne's company initials were monogrammed onto their shirts, and brass stage cannon (for sound effects) backstage were polished daily. The money poured in and Browne, unable to believe he was at last a success, suddenly became unbearably grand. The *Telegraph* critic W. A. Darlington recalled that a colleague had tried to interview both Browne and George V in one week and found that of the two the King was more available.[33]

The show packed houses at the Savoy (its capacity then was a thousand) from where it transferred after three months to the Prince of Wales theatre. Half a million saw it in London alone. Within a year of its opening *Journey's End* had been performed by seventy-six companies in twenty-five languages, including Japanese. In Germany it was a massive hit called *Die Andere Seite* (*The Other Side*), staged at the Deutsches Künstlertheater in Berlin and subsequently by forty other companies in the country. Albert Einstein saw it and loved it. The 1931 German film version starred the great Conrad Veidt as Hauptmann Stanhope and Theodor Loos as Oberleutnant Osborne. Every European capital featured the show. There were five touring companies in America, plus a touring company each in Newfoundland, South Africa, Australia, the West Indies and India. Maurice Browne had within weeks become the most powerful theatre magnate in Europe (by his own account) with a suite of expensive offices. In 1930 the Elmhirsts and he bought the adjacent Globe and Queen's Theatres in Shaftesbury Avenue for £300,000. Browne launched a series of theatre ventures, notably Paul Robeson in

33   George Walter Bishop, *My Betters*, p.43

Othello, in which he disastrously cast himself as Iago and got his wife to direct.

The New York production was a lot more relaxed than the birth of the London show. Browne did a deal with the Broadway producer Gilbert Miller, squeezing from him sixty per cent of the net profits from all productions and no share of the film rights. As the play took 1.5 million dollars in the States, it was another huge cash injection for Browne who was by now riding around in a Packard car with a chauffeur and secretaries flapping around him at all times. Miller, moreover, had agreed to an English cast – a gamble for a Broadway play that was already English enough. It was tried out at the Arts Theatre in London and shipped over to New York lock, stock and barrel. In the event, what the Americans saw at the Henry Miller Theatre (today the Stephen Sondheim Theatre) in New York was a replica of the Savoy production, down to the same bully beef tins, whisky bottles and English newspapers which were carefully packed and exported.

Gilbert Miller was no showbiz thug in a suit. He wanted the actors to look right and sound right. He above all wanted to show his Broadway audiences that the experience of the English soldiers fighting in the trenches was no different to that of the American troops. The play opened with Colin Keith-Johnston as Stanhope and Leon Quartermaine as Osborne. The young Jack Hawkins was Hibbert. (Hawkins acknowledged this break thirty years later when starring as the master criminal in the film *The League of Gentleman;* he and his fellow bank robbers meet in rented rooms, their cover story being that they are actors rehearsing *Journey's End*.) The play triumphed all over again running for 485 performances. One paper hailed the play as the 'best ambassador ever sent to America by Britain.'

Browne had realised his ambition to try and forge a new Anglo-American understanding through the play – part of his internationalist peace agenda. Sherriff's ambitions were much simpler. 'I wanted a fine car that would glide smoothly through the English country lanes, security that would bring me peace of mind, and a farm with cornfields that ran down to the sea.'[34] He got all three and ended up much happier than Browne who never had another success, blew his fortune and died in an orgy of self-pity in 1955.

But Browne always had a sense of purpose for the play and a decided and clear view of its meaning. It was to him a peace play, or at least a play against war. Sherriff doesn't seem to have discussed it with him. The author in a brief article for the *Daily Express* laid out his own view: 'Let me make myself clear. I have not written this play as a piece of propaganda. And certainly not as propaganda for peace. Neither have I tried to glorify the life of the soldier, nor to point to any kind of moral. It is simply the expression of a kind of ideal. I wanted to perpetuate the memory of some of those men.'[35] In his autobiography he was baffled by Maurice Browne's interest in the play.

What made him fall for the play was a mystery to me then, and has remained a mystery ever since. It was totally unlike anything he had produced before, and the sentiments of the characters towards the war were in absolute contrast with his own. They were simple unquestioning men who fought the war because it seemed the only right and proper thing to do. Somebody had got to fight it, and they had accepted the misery and suffering without complaint.[36]

But that is not how others saw it. *Journey's End* was a brilliant indictment of the futility of war and as a protest against it. J.B. Priestley thought it was a plea for peace. Only the *New Statesman* complained about the 'orgy of public school spirit' which turned the war into 'a slaughter-house for athletes and a school for gentlemen.'[37] By not inveighing against the war but by evoking its reality, many critics assumed that Sherriff had thought the best way to condemn the war was not to condemn the war. The *Evening Standard* thought that it appealed to its

34 R.C.S., *No Leading Lady*, p.133
35 SHC, ref 2332
36 *No Leading Lady*, p.72
37 *New Statesman*, 2 February 1929

audience's experience, that they could recall the trenches through the action and be thankful that it was only a play. Their relief was that ' their boots were not wet and their clothes muddy, that their heads no longer wore shrapnel helmets, and it would not be their turn in a few minutes to go up those steps at the back of the stage into the dawn of March 21, 1918, the hiss and slap of machine gun bullets, and the brutal thuddings of bombs. Relief that actuality had at last become only a memory, that could, after 'ten years' delay, finally find its solution in a work of art.'[38]

Sherriff knew he was indebted to the passionate Browne and his burning idealism. Also he was grateful to Agate and after a year of full houses, offered him lunch to thank him for his sterling support. Agate agreed, 'provided I choose the restaurant, I choose the food and, emphatically, I choose the wine.' When the truly eye-watering bill arrived Sherriff picked it up without an intake of breath. George Bishop recalled that the show's success had ruined Browne. 'He lost his head; Bob Sherriff kept his, and he remains today the same charming, unspoiled person whom I met first at the rehearsals of *Journey's End*.'[39]

38 *The Evening Standard*, 22 January 1929
39 G.W.B., *My Betters*, p.48

Civvy Street

One explanation for the play's extraordinary success is that women loved it and they made up a good deal of its audience. Soon after it opened, the *Daily Mail*, ever sensitive to its female readers, ran a piece headlined 'Women Thrilled By Dug Out Dramas' by James Dunn, a war veteran. 'What a lot we talked about food… This talk of food interests the women in the audience. They see men keeping house, and they smile at the well-meant efforts of the mess cook, the tragedy of no pepper, the importance of tinned pineapple over tinned apricots, and the pervading influence of onions on tea.'[40]

Sherriff also explained how the show seemed to have a magnetic pull. 'Women recognized their sons, their brothers or their husbands, many of whom had not returned. The play made it possible for them to journey into the trenches and share the lives that their men had led. For this I could claim no personal credit. I wrote the play the way it came, and it just happened by chance that the way I wrote it was the way people wanted it.'[41]

The only person I interviewed who saw the show in 1929 was Rosemary Price, mother of the late Jill Fraser who ran the Watermill Theatre in Berkshire. 'I was nineteen and it was the first serious show I had been taken to,' she said. 'People were still very emotional about the war. They saw an aspect they hadn't seen before which was the life in the trenches, it was very shocking to see the conditions under which they had to live. It must have been the first time most people realised what a horrible situation the men were in. I remember it was sordid. I also heard a lot of sniffing – the whole theatre was in tears. I fell in love with Colin Clive – I think a lot of us did!'

The author Rebecca West was one of the few women to have written about the play at the time. She saw it four times

40 *Daily Mail* 19 February 1929
41 R.C.S., *No Leading Lady*, p.109

before deciding she didn't like it. She saw it as a play very like *Young Woodley* and *Prisoners of War* in being full of young men having schoolgirl crushes or 'raves' as she called them. 'They all have this obsession with immaturity,'[42] she wrote. The play reminded her just how young the soldiers were. When Stanhope and Raleigh arrived at the front they were eighteen. Sherriff gave us the two extremes of survival at the front – Raleigh lasted less than a week, Stanhope three years. *Journey's End* became a West End memorial for all those boys who hadn't returned as well as a point of reunion for those that had. It also gained from one simple fact: after the war there were no war graves in Britain to visit and tend. This was due to the amazingly progressive decision that the dead would all remain in France and Flanders whatever their families' wishes in the matter. The Imperial War Graves Commission also democratically mixed all ranks together.

The cemeteries – several were designed by Gertrude Jekyll who set their homely pattern – are to this day exquisitely kept with English flowers and shrubs in the flowerbeds. The silence in them is deafening. Kipling came up with the simple words carved on each of the headstones of the unidentified: 'A Soldier of the Great War – Known Unto God.' This is in stark contrast to the French war graves where the missing get a nasty concrete cross with a metal plaque with one word – *inconnu*.

Sherriff returned to the Front as a visitor in the early Twenties. He brought into his play the idea of some sort of dramatic communion with the war dead – and he did it while largely avoiding charges of writing emotional dope. His play, like the cemeteries, became a focal point for veterans and war widows. On the night before Armistice Day 1929 the show was staged exclusively for holders of the Victoria Cross (628 were won in the war, one man winning it twice) and their wives. The evening was a great success although one sergeant overdid it in the bar before the play and stood to attention every time the Colonel made an appearance on stage. On Armistice Day itself *Journey's End* was broadcast by the BBC despite opposition from

42 Rebecca West, *Ending in Earnest*, p.49

Lord Reith who thought the play had too many bangs in it. The *Radio Times* ran a dull full-page appreciation of the play by Charles Morgan. The Savoy Theatre became a place of where the war could be relived with just enough laughter to undercut the solemnity of the subject. The play told it like it was without upsetting the applecart with any complicated cynicism.

The success of the show was less explicable to those untouched by the war. A couple of months after it opened, the producer Harry M. Tennent had a champagne lunch with the young Binkie Beaumont, to become his legendary associate. Their conversation included two great theatre mysteries of the day: why the sinister Charles Laughton had ever been cast as the jovial Mr Pickwick and how *Journey's End* was still playing to capacity at the Savoy. 'I just can't understand it. Not a woman in sight and who wants to remember the war?' said Binkie.[43]

He was right to be puzzled. It's true, by and large nobody wanted to remember the war, not even the survivors. The Depression gave officers and men a sort of grim equality. There are many stories of demobbed colonels repairing prams, majors selling door to door, never mind the vast legion of ex-privates in far more dire circumstances. Employers were sick of hearing about war service and, in the case of officers, their man management skills learned in the trenches. Veterans were despised.

Half of the officers in 9/East Surrey would be dead by the mid-1930s, their ends probably hastened by their wounds. The survivors of the war, however, were a huge problem that wouldn't go away. In 1928-29, the year of the play, some 65,000 veterans were still shaking in mental hospitals. Men had returned home with altered personalities – sullen or facetious – often unrecognisable to their families. Most were prone to sudden tears. Down on the Embankment you could find no shortage of Stanhopes and Raleighs who had long since climbed inside a bottle, their medals pawned and war gratuities blown. There's a piercing description by historian Hugh Cecil of an imaginary

---

43   Richard J. Huggett, *Binkie Beaumont*, p.88

group of ex-officers hanging around in the bar of a peeling South Kensington hotel, drinking gin-and-it with vague dreams of starting a casino or a nightclub. 'Untrained save for giving orders, killing and being killed, they were an embarrassment that most people preferred to forget.'[44]

The war had not been successfully swept under the carpet by the hectic gaiety of the Twenties because the carpet wasn't anything like big enough. The theatre profession was a haven for ex-soldiers. Sherriff never detailed his cast's collective military past but it was quite astonishing. The original *Journey's End* team had more real-life battle experience than any other play before or since. George Zucco (playing Osborne) was in the West Yorkshire regiment and wounded in a raid at St Quentin where the play is set. The chunky Melville Cooper (Trotter) was with the Seaforth Highlanders and had also been taken prisoner of war. James Whale, the director, was captured when as an officer he led an assault on an enemy pillbox and walked into a German trap. David Horne (Captain Hardy) had been a captain in the Grenadier Guards and was wounded in battle. Alexander Field (Mason, the cook) wore the same puttees on stage as he had worn in the trenches. H. G. Stoker (a relative of *Dracula* author Bram Stoker) played the Colonel. Stoker got the DSO as commander of the first submarine to get through the Dardanelles. He was attacked by an Ottoman torpedo boat, scuttled his vessel and was taken to a prison camp where, like Whale, he devised shows for the chaps. By 1928 these men were jobbing actors glad of a total of £5, which is what the Stage Society paid them for three weeks' work. It's a safe bet that one or two of these war veterans knew what it was like to go hungry between acting jobs.

What did the cast secretly think of their producer who emerged from the war unscathed? One wonders. Sherriff was always polite about his producer to whom on one level he was deeply grateful for turning his play into an international smash. But he must have been struck by the irony of having his war

---

44   Hugh Cecil, *The Flower of Battle*, p.269

play produced by a conscientious objector who had stayed safely in America for the duration. 'One would have thought, in the circumstances, that he would have had a violent revulsion against a war play, in which no word of condemnation was uttered by any of its characters,' mused Sherriff.[45]

---

45 R.C.S., *No Leading Lady*, pp.72-73

War Bunk

T he novel of *Journey's End* was, according to the 1930 *Publisher and Bookseller*, 'easily the most popular book throughout the year.' It was co-written by Sherriff and Vernon Bartlett.[46] The novel was immediately lumped with other books that exposed the war. The so-called 'war books' controversy referred to an outpouring of fiction during 1928 –1930 in which the war was massively debunked. It was a sensational period. The top books were Edmund Blunden's *Undertones of War*, *All Quiet on the Western Front* by Erich Maria Remarque, *Death of a Hero* by Richard Aldington, *A Farewell to Arms* by Ernest Hemingway, *Memoirs of an Infantry Officer* by Siegfried Sassoon, *Her Privates We* by Frederic Manning and *Good-bye to All That* by Robert Graves.

They are none of them quite as anti-war as was made out. But they reflected a deep disenchantment (the watch word for the movement) and they all took pains to highlight the cock-ups, the pettiness, the fear. Literary experts have never really explained why 1929 was such a flowering. But it was certainly coloured by a massive disappointment with a country that, ten years after the war was broke, depressed and far from being a land fit for heroes. It was a highly readable genre. It even started to become cannibalistic. The author of the anonymous memoir *War Is War*, Alfred Burrage, admitted to having seen *Journey's End* nine times. As with *Phantom of the Opera* today, a portion of *Journey's End*'s profits can be ascribed to repeat business from customers who were addicted.

Sherriff was no war debunker. His play was seen as pacifist partly because it belonged to an era of peace obsession. In 1926 there was a great anti-war rally at the Royal Albert Hall. The

---

46 Author and broadcaster, Bartlett interviewed Hitler three times. He was an MP from 1938-1950.

independent Labour party issued a pamphlet *How To End War* and a large number of peace organisations had sprung up.

But the play really acquired its peace credentials through association with its great rival, the German novel *All Quiet on the Western Front*. The two works were huge cultural events – global crazes in fact – and at exactly the same time. *All Quiet* was about nineteen-year-old Paul Baumer and a group of five friends who go off to war on a tide of civilian fervour and patriotic duty only to experience the horrors and pointless battles of the front. The enemy turns out not to be the soldiers in the opposing trench but war itself.

The similarities between the two authors' careers, is uncanny. Remarque, two years younger than Sherriff, was wounded by shrapnel and invalided out of the war just two days before him. London caught *Journey's End* fever in January 1929. Ten days after it opened Germany greeted the publication of *All Quiet on the Western Front* with the same clamour. The book sold 20,000 copies a day and notched up a million sales by the end of the year. *All Quiet*, like *Journey's End*, was translated into every European language. Remarque was asked to translate *Journey's End* for the German stage. Sherriff was asked to write the English screenplay for *All Quiet*. Both refused for very different reasons. Remarque admired the play but couldn't face any more war or any more controversy. Sherriff refused because he had promised his mother he'd get back home from New York to go over wallpaper choices for the new house. The two men never met, though Sherriff would eventually work on the screenplay for *The Road Back*, the butchered film sequel to *All Quiet on the Western Front*.

All Quiet's reputation survives partly because it became a masterpiece of American cinema. Directed by Lewis Milestone with a screenplay co-written by George Abbott (later of *Pajama Game* fame), it won Best Picture Oscar for 1930 and made a star out of Lew Ayres as Baumer. The battle scenes have never been bettered. It was the *Saving Private Ryan* of its day. During a French charge the soldiers fall in breaking waves, the German trench finally being overrun where the men fight hand-to-hand with entrenching tools. It's savage, gritty, epic, and even eighty years on, a convincing account of what it must have been like. But the real breakthrough was to depict the evil Hun as a terrified teenager.

Journey's End's chin was elevated slightly more nobly. It had a vein of whimsy and the language is more decorous. In that sense it is totally unrealistic despite its reputation for realism. Everyone finishes sentences, which are mostly grammatical unless a Cockney servant is talking. No one swears except for the odd 'bloody'. Swearing was of course a huge fact of life in the trenches among all ranks. One of the best English novels of the war is Frederic Manning's *Her Privates We* (its title taken from a rude pun in Hamlet) and it contains the real Anglo-Saxon of the trenches. The bad language meant that Manning's novel was riddled with asterisks until the 1970s. It was a problem for all war writers who wanted to be true to what they heard in the field. Norman Mailer's compromise in his war book *The Naked and the Dead* (1948) was to have the soldiers use an invented naughty word 'fug'. It backfired. When the wit Dorothy Parker met him she said: 'so you're the guy who can't spell "fuck."'

Sherriff never quoted the swearing he heard in the trenches. He couldn't have even if he had wanted to: the stage censor wouldn't have allowed it. But what he does do so cleverly is to weave an emotional reality into the text that is so true it doesn't matter that the language is cleaned up and the tragedy softened with pathos. It is partly the atmosphere of euphemism that gives the play its grip.

Even so, *Journey's End* did cause a moral outcry. As Sherriff explained in Cambridge at a League of Nations talk in 1930, he met with an upsurge of complaint soon after the great reviews. He was getting fed up, he said, of letters complaining that an officer in his play dropped his aitches or drank too much. 'One could hardly open *The Times* without reading a letter of criticism from a retired brigadier-general in Cheltenham' he said, claiming it was always brigadier-generals who complained loudest. That was not strictly true – his highest-ranking and loudest critic was the superbly moustached Field Marshal Sir George Milne who gave an interview to the *Star* newspaper.[47] Under the headline 'Tommy Is Not A Beast' the stand-first read: 'Where *Journey's End* Is Wrong.' After grudgingly admitting it was a good play, Milne opened fire. 'No young officer would have been treated in the way Lieutenant Hibbert was treated in that. Someone would have said to a fellow like that in the war, 'Look here, my boy, you had better go down the line for a bit for a rest.' No commanding officer would have kept a neurotic in the front line for the sake of his own reputation. And no soldiers would have sat down to a feast in a dugout after a raid in which their comrades have been killed. That is not English and would never have happened. That is why I dislike *Journey's End* and loathe all these war books.' Milne lambasted all those who depicted the soldiers as 'rotters and drunken blackguards.' Who, he wanted to know, was reading all this stuff? 'Only the young men and women who did not go to war. And all it is doing for them is to make their minds dirty – and they are already dirty enough.'

H. T. W. Bousfield suggested a Society for the Prevention of Cruelty to Ideals in a move against the debased values of *Journey's End* – 'the worst exhibition of bad taste this century has ever seen.'[48] Mussolini was to be congratulated in banning it in Italy and for spotting that the play's conclusion was that 'there was no such thing as heroism.'

In a 1930 profile in *Good Housekeeping*, *The Observer* critic and playwright St. John Ervine, who lost a leg in the war fighting with the Dublin Fusiliers, recalled that he had met Sherriff on board ship while crossing the Atlantic and that he struck him as decent. 'I instantly liked him. His unaffected boyish manner was very attractive… Mr Sherriff to me, is almost the embodied spirit of all subalterns. He is what we mean when we talk of the gallant lads who went out

47   *Star*, 26 March 1930
48   *English Review*, October 1929

to the War and never came back from it. I cannot think of any person who more closely typifies the subaltern than Mr Sherriff does. Except that Sherriff didn't drink much.

Most officers drank heavily. Of course they did. Ervine went on to say, in the same piece, how no one got used to the war in a paragraph that Sherriff might have written himself. 'The longer one served on the front, the worst one felt the strain...that young officers, nerve-racked and frightened, were more terrified of showing funk before their men than they were of meeting Germans and that to pull themselves together, they took a tot, then two tots, then several tots, to keep up their courage; that in the time of intense strain, the whisky bottle gave comfort to men who had a continuous rendez-vous with death; and that in the first shock of losing comrades, men shed tears freely and easily.'

Whisky is the cause of a long discussion very early in the play. Hardy says to Osborne: 'the last time we were resting out at Valennes he [Stanhope] came to supper with us and drank a whole bottle in one hour fourteen minutes – we timed him.' (Act I) Stanhope is described as a 'freak' for his consumption. But it was not that unusual. When Stanhope says 'If I went up those steps into the front line – without being doped with whisky – I'd go mad with fright', he spoke for just about every officer in the frontline. When a society hostess lambasted Noël Coward about *Journey's End*, saying it was a vile libel on the army and that officers didn't drink, Coward merely turned to his friend Earl Amherst, who had been an officer in the trenches, and asked what he thought. 'Never drew a sober breath,' said the earl.

But despite the outbursts and the depiction of alcoholism, swearing and funk, the play was at heart deeply acceptable. Unlike *All Quiet*, it didn't decry militarism. Sherriff didn't really have a pacifist bone in his body. His story simply married up a tale of sporting hero-worship, one that had been doing the rounds in British culture for a few decades, with a realistic trench setting. It worked like a dream. It rapidly became a national possession and was deemed suitable to be seen by George V (monarch and playwright chatted at the interval), a sure sign it contained nothing to frighten the horses. Winston Churchill loved it. As Chancellor of the Exchequer, he invited Sherriff to 11 Downing Street. Churchill had been an officer in the trenches and knew all about the 9/East Surrey. He watched the play very carefully and before their meeting he fired off some probing questions by letter – eg. why did Stanhope write a note and send it down the line to Battalion HQ? Did it contain Osborne's ring and letters for safekeeping? Why did the Sergeant-Major think it odd that Mr Raleigh when wounded should be brought into the company's dugout? Sherriff in his autobiography admits he didn't really know the answers to the Chancellor's questions.[49]

The Establishment embraced the play. It was a piece of theatre that unified the public in an agreed memory of what the war was like. Audiences went home gratefully enlightened, informed and deeply moved. It celebrated traditional values of honour and loyalty and it was consoling, which later earned it powerful enemies. St. John Ervine's one criticism was of the play's immaturity of thought and 'foolish worship of the public school that has been excessively prevalent in the country for too long a time.'[50] Sherriff's play was indeed an extension of the public school life that Rebecca West complained about. Raleigh worships Stanhope, describing him as 'skipper of rugger at Barford, and kept wicket for the Eleven. A jolly good bat, too!' He is delighted when he discovers that Osborne once played rugby for the Harlequins and on one sacred occasion for England. Before the raid it is Raleigh who says 'how topping if we both get MC!' Raleigh is but a whisker away from *Blackadder's* Lieutenant the Honourable George Colthurst St. Barleigh who wants to give 'Harry Hun a darn good British style thrashing, six of the

49   R.C.S., *No Leading Lady*, p.113
50   *Good Housekeeping*, 1930

best, trousers down.' Edward Petherbridge played Osborne in a 1988 TV version of the play shown on BBC2 (with Jeremy Northam as Stanhope) and gave a flicker of a smile at Raleigh's gushing school banter. It's a lovely silent comment on Raleigh's Sherriff-like naivety.

Sherriff didn't have a problem with depicting the war – or bits of it – as a school yarn albeit one soured by alcohol and death. But the play's youthfulness may explain why it has fared so badly at the hands of literary historians. You hardly ever read a good word about the play in books about the literature of the period. War Poetry expert Bernard Bergonzi hated it. He wrote 'the inert clichés of Sherriff's final stage direction emphasize the kind of predictable experience we have just passed through: "very faintly comes the rattle of machine guns and the fevered spatter of rifle fire."'[51]

Two landmark surveys of First World War literature are by American scholars, both of them decorated soldiers of World War Two. Paul Fussell wrote the classic *The Great War and Modern Memory* (1975) and Samuel Hynes *A War Imagined: The First World War and English Culture* (1990). Fussell's book is a haunting scholastic delve into the literary riches of the war (*Les Misérables* lyricist Herbert Kretzmer chose it as his book on Desert Island Discs) but it utterly dismisses *Journey's End* and cites its importance only in giving Joseph Heller an idea for a similar death scene in *Catch-22*.

Hynes is much ruder and equally brief. He thought it recycled a bunch of trench stereotypes – the coward, the officer who drinks to forget, the naïve schoolboy-officer etc. What he most disliked was the analogy between the world of the trenches and the world of the British public schools. 'There is the same idolizing, the same adolescent emotionalism, the same team spirit and self-sacrifice, the same hovering note of homosexuality. That model of behaviour – so English, so male,

---

51   Bernard Bergonzi, *Heroes' Twilight*, p.194

and so anachronistic – was killed on the Western Front. In Sherriff's play it was resurrected and sentimentalised.'[52]

He is right about the sentimentality. It is the play's famous weakness. But the front-line dugout was a curiously sentimental place. As for the sporting gentleman, he was certainly not killed off on the Western Front. World War Two had loads of nonchalant British POWs wearing cricket sweaters who treated escape as a team sport. The spirit of heroism, pluck and understatement in the trenches lived on in films, books and in reality. It is even possible that the fighter pilots in 1940 acquired some of their fondness for understatement from *Journey's End*.

Sherriff didn't invent the schoolboy spirit he found out there in France. He simply drew on it. If you weren't a public school boy officer you did your level best to behave like one, as Sherriff did. As for the 'hovering note of homosexuality,' Sherriff's was crush-prone and it shows in the play. Raleigh – with his aristocratic name and unsullied youth – is arguably one of the 'golden lads' that a lot of dubious trench poetry is taken with. You could also say that the drunken Stanhope, when he asks Osborne to tuck him up at night and kiss him has something further on his mind. I think to ascribe any sexuality to the play is to miss the point. Sherriff was always thinking of England.

Whatever it was that made it a hit, the 1930 film version proved a death sentence for the London run. Whale was recruited by the independent Tiffany Studios to make his directing debut on it with Gainsborough Studios. George Pearson, the famed British director of the silent era was the supervisor and he wanted Olivier to play Stanhope. But Whale, as director, insisted that Colin Clive go to California and make the picture. Browne agreed provided he took just eight weeks out of the play and not a day more. The deal was that he returned to the show by mid-January 1930. I have been unable to find out who took over his role. But whoever it was, it was a mistake. Clive had become the show's heart-throb star, the reason for seeing the show and Sherriff knew it: 'So far as London was concerned, Colin

---

52   Samuel Hynes, *A War Imagined*, p.442

Clive *was Journey's End.*[53] He begged Browne not to let him go. Clive went.

The film was well received. Mordaunt Hall reviewing for *The New York Times* wrote, 'On the whole Mr. Clive's performance is magnificent. Even in the close-ups his facial expressions are perfectly in keeping with the mood of the moment.' Edward C. Stein of *The Brooklyn Standard Union* thought, 'His performance of the nerve-wracked, whiskey-soaked, yet thoroughly admirable captain defies superlatives. The part is made to order for him and if you miss seeing his portrayal you are missing one of the finest performances of this or any other season.'

Speaking of the role, Clive in the July 1931 issue of *Theatre World* modestly said that 'Stanhope was so beautifully written and effective it almost played itself. Any experienced actor could have walked away with it.' Looking at the film version, you get an idea of Clive's sense of physical strain, the rasping voice and baleful good looks in his close-ups. But the film feels hammy rather than dramatic, the director Whale perhaps hampered by a loyalty to his own stage production. The movie version never really took off, though within a year Clive would achieve screen stardom in *Frankenstein* (1931), hysterically shouting 'it's ali-i-i-i-vvve!' as his monster (Boris Karloff) twitches on the bench. Osborne – that's to say George Zucco – also went onto screen fame in a series of lurid shockers, often involving zombies.

Back in London, news of Clive's temporary departure got around and the box office dipped. Soon the House Full boards were removed from the pavement and the audience shrank. Clive returned to the show but the spell was broken. The audiences slowly withered away and it eventually closed after a run of 593 performances – a record-breaking stint at the time for a straight play. The writer and cast toasted New Year behind the lowered curtain. The dugout must have begun to smell like the real thing.

53   R.C.S., *No Leading Lady*, p.191

The Cold Front

One reason given for the play's success is that there was no rival to the play. In fact *Journey's End* is part of a triptych of plays set in 1918, two of them on the same day. *Havoc* was a substantial hit five years before Sherriff's – and one wonders if he didn't see it. Originally at the Regent Theatre in 1923, Harry Wall's play successfully transferred to the Haymarket the following year. Like *Journey's End* it was turned into both a novel and a film. Unlike Sherriff's play, it has women in the cast – notably a heartless society bitch played (at the Haymarket) by Frances Carson. The plot revolved around two officers in love with this femme fatale. The front-line scenes are identical to *Journey's End* and the quality of the ration meat is no better. 'It's supposed to be bit of a cow,' ventures one officer on his brown plateful. The whisky consumption is about the same too. The handsome young subaltern Playfair is called 'The Babe' and the Stanhope-like officer Roddy Chappell is considered 'awfully fit, and simply splendid in the line.'

The play uses a lot of army slang, much more than Sherriff's. Being scared is having 'beaucoup wind up' and an attack is a 'stunt.' In the dugout, Roddy finds his engagement broken off by Violet who returns him her ring. He then sends his comrade and love rival, Dick, and seventeen volunteers to what looks like certain death as the Germans attack. In the event the plan doesn't work: Dick is blinded but not killed and Roddy does the decent thing and shoots himself. The play is deeply melodramatic but it clearly kept audiences gripped. The shelling is heavy – sound effects would have been a big feature of the piece – and there is plenty of trench action where the atmosphere of the front line is recreated. The women's frocks – *Play Pictorial* did a lavish photo-spread – were a vital part of its success at a time when managements considered the war a clapped-out subject. The title referred not to the battle scenes but the damage done to the male heart in the midst of war.

The other play set against the backdrop of the German offensive of 1918 was called *Suspense* – a title that along with *Waiting* Sherriff had considered for his own play – and it was clearly indebted to *Journey's End*, opening after it at the Duke of York's in 1930. The difference being that the play's author Patrick MacGill, known as the 'navvy poet', was a great champion of the working class ('press agent to the Common Man' as *The Times* called him) and his soldiers were privates. The sound of an enemy mine being dug throughout the show provides the suspense and all the action is concentrated into the last five brilliant minutes. The exhausted unit is making its way back to safety from the front along the duckboards. A mine goes off under the trenches they have just left and the enemy attacks with gas and shrapnel. Thinking they were winding their way out of the line for six blissful days, they are ordered to attack and the play closes with them advancing and dropping one by one in a shroud of mist. But the war was to produce only one front-line play that took off. Sherriff had caught the spirit of the front and its human cost all in one go. It had done its job and when it closed the play was suddenly very old hat.

Sherriff toyed with the idea of writing a play about the South Pole. Like his thwarted explorer father, he was utterly fascinated by the story of Scott. The expedition was seen as inspirational to a pre-war generation thirsty for heroism. Schools everywhere pinned up in their corridors Scott's last words written from his tent. 'Had we lived, I should have had a tale to tell of the hardihood, courage of my companions which would have stirred the heart of every Englishman...'

As he was dying, Scott wrote from his tent. 'I do not regret this journey, which has shown that Englishmen can endure hardships, help one another, and meet death with as great a fortitude as ever in the past.' That is pretty much the spirit that is summoned up in Sherriff's dugout. Osborne is a reluctant Oates. Sherriff never writes about his play as a reaction of the Scott expedition. But it was in the air. Immediately after *Journey's End* he put it about that he was thinking of working on a polar play, though he never wrote anything, perhaps out of fear of Scott's rather scary widow. Also, perhaps, because he was beaten to the pole by playwright Frank Harvey, whose *The Last Enemy* ran at the Fortune Theatre from the end of 1929 for several weeks, a struggling rival to *Journey's End*, set in the Antarctic.

It might be a companion piece to Sherriff's play. Its plot features two Antarctic explorers, marooned in the frozen wastes. Dr McKenzie is forty-four and the younger explorer is the twenty-two-year-old Jimmy Churchill, mad keen on 'rugger'. It is September 1896 and they are waiting in vain for the rescue party. The men have eschewed the morphine pills and are facing the end. By the end of Act One the pair are on their way to heaven.

The next act is set in 1916, Laurence Olivier (fresh from the flopped *Beau Geste* play) playing Jerry Warrender, a pilot in the Flying Corps, age twenty-eight and halfway to a nervous breakdown, living on a strict diet of whisky. He is described as 'war mad – nerves all gone to pot'. In the last act one of the the polar heroes becomes a guardian angel to a wounded character lying in a shell hole on the Somme. The dead and the living mingle on stage. In the play Olivier, who had missed out on playing Stanhope in the West End transfer, got his chance to play the alcoholic officer who drinks to forget the brutal reality of war.

What is so fascinating is the bizarre collision of themes, authors and actors. Sherriff idolised James Barrie, the author of *Peter Pan*. Barrie cherished his friendship with Captain Scott who wrote to him from his tent in his very last days. In 1930 Barrie was a virtual hermit living in a desolate-sounding flat in Adelphi Terrace. Sherriff, newly famous, paid him a visit. The prospect of meeting his hero was a great thrill. But the dwarfish Scotsman kept his back to him and said virtually not a word having passed his guest a cup of tea and a chunk of inedible fruitcake. He sat so still and with his back to Sherriff that the young author began to wonder whether he had died. 'The only part of him I could see was the top of his head. He had a big pear shaped head, very broad at the top, with a few wisps of brown hair brushed across it. I wondered whether I ought to touch it to find out whether it had gone cold.'[54] It's a comic set piece in his autobiography, Sherriff relishing the banality of the encounter and not questioning Barrie's rudeness. But I think the grieving Barrie literally couldn't face him. He had lost his adopted son George Llewlyn Davies (a death he foresaw) at the Front and Sherriff was simply the wrong young officer in the room.

Sherriff would have known and admired the lecture on Courage that Barrie gave the Rectorial Address at St Andrews University in 1922, which was published in a popular small volume. Bracco in *Merchants of Hope* draws attention to his very Barrie-ish story about an Alpine expedition. A group of young friends go climbing and one of them falls down a crevasse to his death. His bereaved friends work out the date long in the future when the glacier will yield up his body. Decades on, the party, now old, returns at the predicted time and there preserved in the ice is the body, as young as the day they left him. 'So Scott and his comrades emerge from the white immensities always young,' spoke Barrie to the students.

Is *Journey's End* a hymn to eternal youth, preserved out there in France, defending a trench? Perhaps the play is an attempt to relocate Scott's tent on the Western Front? Scott wrote to Barrie with frostbitten fingers: 'We are in a desperate state – feet frozen etc., no fuel, and a long way from food, but it would do your heart good to be in our tent, to hear our songs and our cheery conversation.'[55]

It's as if the whole thing was a school expedition gone hideously wrong. Sherriff includes enough school references to suggest the same about the officer's dugout where death awaits the inhabitants. Its morbidity is very much of its time. According to Peter Parker's book *The Old Lie*, Peter Pan's famous line 'to die would be an awfully big adventure' was discreetly dropped

54   R.C.S., *No Leading Lady*, p.179
55   J.M. Barrie, *Courage*, p.31 cited in Bracco

from performances of the play in 1916 presumably because it was getting sneers of derision from soldiers on leave who knew the reality. But Sherriff could easily have assigned that line to Raleigh at the start of the play. Raleigh arrives not wanting to die but not minding too much if he does, providing there's a chance of winning the MC.

Sherriff's vision of the officers around him was one of children playing at soldiers. In his diary he wrote that on his very first night in a trench he wondered how many others like him were 'standing about awkwardly like children in a drawing room – fingering their new revolver holsters and remembering the time (not so distant) when they last wore weapons as pirates or brigands defending a summerhouse in the garden.'

Sherriff never dramatised the life of Scott, though he did produce an essay on him for a 1933 anthology called *The Post-Victorians*. It is a brief account of his rise to fame and too short to reveal anything of Sherriff's own interest in the man. 'To quote passages from Scott's last diary is akin to hacking pieces from a perfect memorial,' he wrote with unthinking adoration. Sherriff's worship was immune to the great Scott debunk led by Bernard Shaw who called him 'the most incompetent failure in the history of exploration.' Captain Scott went through the same character assassination as the Great War itself – a tale of ineptitude, imperialistic pride and culpable homicide.

One hundred years on it is Captain Oates who today has the limelight. His self-sacrifice is now arguably the heart of the South Pole story, not Scott's drive and leadership. Oates was tough as old boots but in that fatal blizzard he knew he had it. Stooping out of the tent with the immortal words 'I may be some time,' he trudged into the screaming blizzard. In his socks. In *Journey's End*, Osborne's reaction to his orders – he knows it's a death sentence – is to say 'righto.' Religion plays no part in the play but Osborne strikes me as the most deeply Christian character. He goes on the raid knowing he will be killed but some external courage invades him and (with the additional help of Lewis Carroll) he finds he can go over the top.

Barrie seemed to have genuinely believed that the dead and the living were divided by the thinnest veil of gauze. Sherriff didn't, for him, the dead lived on only in the land of memory. That's the landscape he created for them on stage. Sherriff stayed as young as the men he left behind in France. Sherriff was always young, even in his pictures in middle age. In his autobiography, written when he was seventy-two, he sounds about nineteen. Like Barrie, there is something decidely weird about his immunity to ageing.

It is typical that when Sherriff returned home he bought with his war gratuity a new sculling boat and a set of English history books to read in the evenings. When his play became a hit, the press naturally wanted to know what he was like. So he wrote a piece for *Pictorial Weekly* with the headline 'I Believe in Simplicity'[56] which outlined – at slightly tedious length – his philosophy of being as natural and as unpretentious as possible.

His next play was *Badger's Green*, a simple comedy about a simple village divided and made miserable by far from simple developers. Sherriff added a cricket match around which the action revolved. It has a good first act and then it goes to pot. Like *Journey's End* it was directed by Whale and produced by Browne. It flopped largely because, as Agate privately pointed out, it had no machine guns, sandbags or explosions and that's what folk were expecting. It is certainly not unlikeable though, and two film versions followed in 1934 and 1949.

It was not the end of *Journey's End* however, as Sherriff planned a prose sequel. The play was still in his mind and he drafted an outline for a novel that would chime with the economic slump and also provide an afterlife for his hero Captain Stanhope who it turns out was not killed at St Quentin as we thought.

The action picks up the very second the play ends with Stanhope going up into the trench at the start of the great barrage. Clinging onto the ruined trenches, he finds himself surrounded and cut off by the enemy. At dawn, he is asked by the Germans to surrender and he vaingloriously refuses. The

56 *Pictorial Weekly*, 29 November 1930

shelling starts until just a few of his men remain and he is concussed and wakes up to find his doughty companion and second-in-command Trotter beside him. They are taken to a prisoner-of-war camp where Stanhope is avoided by the other men for his moroseness, brought on by a dread of returning home. He still dreams of returning to his sweetheart Madge, his mind unsullied by the war.

Once back, he tries to get a post with a City financier who once promised him a job. He is politely refused. His war record is much appreciated – but he is useless. It's the same story everywhere. Driven by poverty, he goes to the Ex-Officers' Employment Bureau and accepts a job as a travelling salesman for a new venture – Ramsay's Custard Powder. Instead of rebuilding the Britain he fought for, as he dreamed on his return, he is trudging the streets with samples of 'Ramcust', ingratiating himself with small grocers, living in dread of meeting old friends as he tramps the streets.

At the end of his tether, he bumps into a former sergeant who was in his company in France. The sergeant and the workers are planning a strike in a steelworks where they have been badly treated. Stanhope sides with them in the pub. He is determined the men shall have justice – he plans the strike strategy as he would a trench raid, a bottle of whisky by his side. When the confrontation comes at the factory gates he is hopelessly defeated by the young manager's logic in having to let some of the workers go. Having lost the argument and the respect of the men he represents, Stanhope slopes off to his lodging and turns on the gas. Even his suicide fails. Eventually, the industrialist hears of his plight and takes pity. Sherriff wrote: 'They had hoped that the war would harden them into men of tremendous value in the fight for peace and prosperity, but instead the war had sucked them dry of all the forces Youth had given them.'[57]

Stanhope ends up with a job running Sports and Recreations for the company he planned to strike against. 'Just as, in the War,

57   SHC, ref 2332

it was not the Germans who were the enemy, but some great unseen evil that both Germans and his own men fought against together? Quite what the evil is he never explains. But clearly the one character he couldn't let go of was Stanhope. Captain Godfrey Warre-Dymond was the man Sherriff acknowledged as the model for this character.

Warre-Dymond – the battle-hardened name sounds too good to be true – was born in 1890 and educated at Marlborough and Cambridge and seems to have been exactly the sort of athletic Varsity man young Raleigh in the play would have worshipped. Michael Lucas has researched his background as one of the most notable officers of the 9/East Surrey. He arrived on the Somme in August 1916 and entered Sherriff's battalion in September. He was in charge of C Company from March 1917. He won the MC and was mentioned in dispatches three times. He was not killed, but taken prisoner in 1918 at the battalion's last stand. There is evidence of an unsettled life after the war, of exactly the sort that the fictional Stanhope might have lived. He was even sacked from the family auctioneering firm by his father. He was prosecuted for drunken driving, declared bankrupt in 1923, twice petitioned for divorce, ending up as a commercial traveller, as in Sherriff's story. The bare facts certainly don't suggest domestic bliss or post-war adjustment. On civvy street it was Sherriff who went on to fame and glory while the glamorous war hero became, it seems, a sorry mess.

If Stanhope has a fictional peacetime counterpart, it is Freddy Page, the dashing, hard-drinking, slightly dim ex-Battle-of-Britain fighter pilot in Terence Rattigan's *The Deep Blue Sea* (1952) with whom the respectably married Hester falls disastrously in love. Freddie drinks because, according to Hester, 'his life stopped in 1940. He loved 1940, you know. There were some like that.' Rattigan was himself a wartime airman – he once crashlanded his Sunderland aircraft with the unfinished manuscript of his play *Flare Path* stuffed up his shirt – and knew the type all too well. Freddy was one of Churchill's Few, Stanhope one of Haig's Many. Both in peacetime were superfluous to requirements. But

Sherriff was unable to find a way of putting the characters of *Journey's End* into a convincing peacetime context, so he gave up the story. It would be Noël Coward who wrote the real *Journey's End* sequel.

How *Post-Mortem* came about is worth looking into, as *Journey's End* was its direct inspiration. The link between Coward and Sherriff was a keen young actor John Mills, years before he made it as a film star. According to his autobiography, Mills had been stuck in the chorus of *The Five O'Clock Girl* for eight months when he went for auditions for a Far Eastern tour of *Journey's End* with R. B. Salisbury's company, known (unbelievably) as The Quaints. Mills had seen Maurice Evans play Raleigh three times and fancied himself in the part. To his dismay he was given instead the role of the coward Hibbert to read. By fluke, Sherriff was walking past the theatre that morning and dropped in to watch the audition. 'What's that boy reading Hibbert for? He looks like the perfect Raleigh to me.'[58] Mills got the part he wanted.

By the time the company reached Singapore, Coward had also sailed into town, travelling on a six-month writing jaunt with his friend Earl Amherst. Forced to wait in town for Amherst's recovery from a bout of dysentery, Coward found the company playing at the Victoria Theatre and popped in. *Hamlet* was the play advertised outside the theatre. But as Horatio was found to be drunk following a party at the High Commissioner's earlier that day, they staged *Mr. Cinders* instead. Coward afterwards befriended the company. He offered to take over as Stanhope in *Journey's End* for three performances opposite Mills as Raleigh. This was a great coup for the modest company to have the author of *Hay Fever* and his new smash hit *Private Lives* in their midst.

By most accounts including his own, Coward was terrible in the part, one local critic describing him as a 'whimpering neurotic prig'. On the boat home, he wrote *Post-Mortem* in reaction to *Journey's End*. He called it 'an angry little vilification of war' which purged him of 'certain accumulated acids'. Having

58   John Mills, *Up in the Clouds, Gentlemen Please*, p.53

written it, he was oddly reluctant to get it produced. Coward thought it contained some of his best and worst writing. With war books all the rage, he had tried his hand at what was an overtly political play.

Post-Mortem has eight rapid scenes and one act and starts and ends on the front line in 1917. The company commander is John Cavan, the idealistic, optimistic son of a newspaper editor. His comrade Perry Lomas is more cynical: he believes that the War is a waste of time and no one will learn a thing from it. Cavan is then killed and his spirit fast-forwards into the future, to 1930, to see who was right. Cavan as a ghost meets and talks with those from his past – his still grieving mother, his society fiancée; he interrupts the attempted suicide of his old chum Perry, whose book *Post-Mortem* is savaged by the press for telling the grim truth about the war. He meets his press baron father and finally the men he shared a trench with. In the end he returns to his death. Declaring life a poor joke, the play ends up having denounced the mendacity of the press and the callousness of the peace. Cavan dies lamenting the futility of his generation's sacrifice for a shallow hypocritical present.

Bizarrely, the play was given its first performance in 1944 at a POW camp (Oflag VII-b) in Germany. In the cast were some pre-war professional actors including a young Welch Fusilier, Desmond Llewellyn, later to become famous as Q in the James Bond films. On greeting the text's publication the *Daily Mirror* wrote, 'A fearful study in disillusionment! … The misery is, if I may use a vulgarism, laid on very thick. But there are passion and brave satire in this play. Mr. Coward is to be congratulated. He is always renewing himself. I am afraid, however, that, for the stage, *Post-Mortem* is really too depressing to make another *Journey's End*.'[59]

The play was staged again in 1992 at the King's Head Theatre in London with Sylvia Syms in the cast. Its attack on an England more interested in saluting the dead than caring for its survivors had traction. As for its attack on the press, that too was timely and

---

59 *Daily Mirror*, 23 May 1931

arguably still is considering the recent easy ride the government has had from Fleet Street over the war in Afghanistan (Britain's fourth to date in that country).

Post-Mortem may not be a great play but it was in touch with a new mood. Had it been immediately produced in the West End, it would have left *Journey's End* even more isolated in its lagoon of shells and khaki memories. Coward, having abandoned the play to the bottom drawer, next turned *Journey's End* into a sketch. His 1932 revue *Words and Music* included a truly inspired piss-take of the play that had become an institution. Audiences chortled with pleasure as Stanhope sat drinking champagne by the light of a silver candelabra. 'Three years of this hell. Will it never end. God! I am tired. Only wine can keep me going. God! I am tired, tired, tired.' Raleigh then enters. He is a woman.

Raleigh: 'I came to be near you, Mein Klein Pupchen.'

Raleigh tears off an overcoat, revealing an evening dress of khaki and sequins, and sings. He is followed by a tank, which disgorges twelve leggy chorus girls wearing tin hats. Stanhope bangs on some more about being tired and how 'Only wine can keep me going. Wine and memories.' He then produces a guitar and sings a Spanish serenade and six senoritas appear, clicking castanets. Next some German prisoners enter and they execute a violent slapping dance. In the show was John Mills in Tyrolean costume singing 'Gondolas on the Somme.' To this, add a singing appearance from a British General and the Kaiser with a heavy Scots accent. The whole skit with sequins, balloons and an orchestra playing *Deutschland über alles* was a hugely camp send-up of trench life. Mel Brooks couldn't have done it better.

Coward – with an eye to the box office – at much the same time had written an overtly patriotic panorama of England, *Cavalcade*, charting – like *Upstairs, Downstairs* – a family's fortunes from 1900 to 1929. It featured gassed soldiers in the war sequence. But its bunting and flagwaving revolted Somerset Maugham. Maugham came up with a magnificently bitter and disillusioned play, *For Services Rendered* (1932), about a blinded veteran and the war's effects on an English family. It was re-staged superbly in 1993 by Deborah Paige for the Salisbury Playhouse and ended up at the Old Vic spewing bucketloads of disillusionment gratifyingly over the stage. As with the *Post-Mortem* revival, it featured the venerable Sylvia Syms.

It depicted a family ruined by the war and an England fit for speculators but not heroes. It has an amazingly prophetic outburst by the ex-soldier, Sydney Ardsley. It is the speech that Maurice Browne always wanted to hear and which Sherriff never wrote. 'We were the dupes of the incompetent fools who ruled the nations. I know we were sacrificed to their vanity, their greed and their stupidity. And the worst of it is that as far as I can tell they haven't learnt a thing. They're just as vain, they're just as greedy, they're just as stupid as they ever were. They muddle on, muddle on, and one of these days they'll muddle us into another war.' (Act III)

Maugham as far as I know never castigated *Journey's End* but the show certainly had distinguished enemies. The mightiest was Sean O'Casey (1880-1964), the Irish playwright who had written his own war play, *The Silver Tassie*. The play is about Harry Heegan, winner of a local football cup (the silver tassie of the title) who returns from the war maimed, bitter and in a wheelchair. Harry loses his girl to his best mate who won the VC for saving his life. It is famous for its nightmarish, expressionistic second act – set somewhere in a war zone. The idea was that this hellish, satiric vision of war would contrast with the Dublin scenes and show up the great divide between the front and home life.

The play was the cause of a famous row between O'Casey and W. B. Yeats who rejected the play on behalf of the Abbey Theatre in Dublin. Yeats based his entire objection on O'Casey's lack of direct experience of combat. 'You never stood on its battlefields or walked its hospitals, and so you write out of your opinions', he wrote in a letter.[60] Although it is true O'Casey didn't fight, he had in fact walked the hospitals, having been confined on a Dublin ward full of wounded and

---

60   20 April 1928

dying Irish soldiers. He also knew all about the military. Half his family was in the pre-war army and his brother Mick re-enlisted in 1915. O'Casey had also just written a stunning play about the Easter Rising in 1916. From that it was a short step to a scathing play about the Great War's aftermath. 210,000 Irish troops had served in the war and some 30,000 were killed – the greatest Irish catastrophe since the Famine.

O'Casey's play opened at the Apollo (ten months after *Journey's End* opened there) with Charles Laughton as Harry Heegan and the second act 'warscape' designed by Augustus John. It differs vastly from *Journey's End* in that it has parts for women – mothers, sisters, girlfriends, nurses and so on. O'Casey thought Sherriff's work was offensively sissy: 'The stench of blood hid in a mist of soft-sprayed perfume; the yells of agony modulated down to a sweet pianissimo of pain...all the mighty, bloodied vulgarity of war foreshortened into a petty, pleasing picture', he wrote.[61] He approvingly quoted a remark of the American critic G. J. Nathan's that *Journey's End* depicted 'a ladies' war' and that it 'needed only a butler to convert it into a polite drawing-room comedy'. (Actually, the play doesn't need a butler as it's already got one in Mason, a cockney Jeeves.)

O'Casey doesn't spell it out. But what angered him was perhaps the domesticity of Sherriff's trench. If so, he was onto something. Sherriff's dugout is in many ways as cosy as Mole's home in *The Wind in the Willows*. Stanhope suggests that Osborne wear an apron and 'clean the trenches up with a little dustpan and brush'. Osborne for his part talks of 'something special for dinner'. We could be back in Sherriff's house in Hampton Wick with the kettle whistling and the fire lit. You would hardly know there was a war on or that these people were soldiers. Osborne's line 'Don't forget to throw your bombs' is a handy tip but it does sound rather camp. O'Casey – maybe because he was Irish – didn't get the

61   Sean O'Casey, *Rose and Crown*, p.128

Edwardian tea-time Englishness that Sherriff sought to evoke in his trench.

Geoffrey Streatfeild, who played Stanhope, described the play's domesticity as an aspect of the men's overwhelming need for hearth and home: 'what you have is one monumental silence over two acts and five scenes before the big noise of death at the end. These men try to fill the silence as best they can with little seeds of England. Any time they can civilize the mud hole they are in by having tea or talking about their gardens back home. They seem to say let's bring a little bit of the England we've left behind and we can survive.'[62]

O'Casey, who was reaching out for the searing tragedy of the war, took exception to the play's vein of pathos and its appeal as a souvenir of the war in all its aspects, not just its horrors. He was revolted by the way the men in the play are sustained by memories of home rather than the thought of fighting for a better future. His temper towards Sherriff also can't have been improved by the latter's success. While O'Casey was unquestionably the greater dramatist, Sherriff had by far the bigger hit. He probably earned more from the play than O'Casey earned in his entire lifetime. *The Silver Tassie* was staged by Galway's Druid Theatre Company in 2010; the tour included one week at the Oxford Playhouse. The design had a full-scale model of a tank that filled the stage. It was a terrific visual coup by designer Francis O'Connor. The thing even moved at you. The tank instantly evoked Sassoon's bitter lines about music hall nostalgia and a tank lurching down the stalls to ragtime tunes. But the great demolition of *Journey's End* came a generation after it. Its modernism and tone of withering sarcasm instantly consigned Sherriff's play to the skip of has-been plays.

Oh What A Lovely War was not so much written as made up in rehearsals by Joan Littlewood and her partner Gerry Raffles and the cast of the Theatre Workshop company. It was first staged on 19 March 1963 (in the same week that The Beatles'

62 *The Man from Esher*, BBC Radio 4, 30 March 2006

first LP came out) at their London base at the Theatre Royal, Stratford East. Littlewood hated *Journey's End* even more than O'Casey – if that's possible. The musical was based on Charles Chilton's BBC hugely popular Christmas radio play of 1961 *The Long, Long Trail* which featured many of the songs – given an ironic twist by the soldiers – gathered up in a songbook called *Tommy's Tunes* in 1917. Chilton's father, who Charles never knew, died on the Western Front at the age of nineteen. In trying to find his grave in 1958, Charles was deeply shocked when he came across his name on a wall along with thousands of missing men who died in the Battle of Arras.

It was Littlewood's idea to tell the story of the war through the songs Chilton had rediscovered while a pierrot troupe played out a charade called *The War Game*. (Noël Coward had also used pierrots in his war skit thirty years before.) *Oh What A Lovely War* was miles ahead of its time. It used every avant garde European theatre device going (including a screen with statistics of casualties and yards of ground gained in lights) and saw the war entirely from the point of view of the ranks. It relied on a lot of oral testimony (pre-dating by decades the 'forgotten voices' movement) in its research. The cast brought in bits of homework. A drill sergeant came into rehearsals to lick the men into shape and shocked even the actors with his language. The staging and the sweetness of the period songs gave it – to judge from those who were there – a sensuousness in contrast with the blunt horror of the numbers of dead. Underneath it all was a fury against the ruling elites (the show featured cartoon-like versions of the Kaiser, Lloyd George, Haig and assorted brasshats) who had slaughtered millions to no avail – and were probably about to do so again in a nuclear war.

So why did Joan loathe *Journey's End* so much? The answer is, no one has a clue. She never explained and everyone was too nervous to ask. Her colleague Peter Rankin told me: 'No one could mention the play in front of her. She would explode. Nor would she ever allow the colour khaki near the stage.'

The late Victor Spinetti, who played the show's MC, recalls in his memoir that 'one of the first things she asked us to do was act out what we knew of the First World War. We could be anything from the reminiscences of a relative to films with stiff-upper-lip actors. We even did *Journey's End*, a play Joan so detested, she used to lose her temper when someone simply mentioned it.'[63] The possible reason for her loathing was that it was a play about officers and officers were the groveling lackeys of the system. Sherriff's play utterly conflicted with her Leninist view of the war as a bayonet with a worker at either end. In his book *The Great War* the author Dan Todman quotes an interview Littlewood gave in *Tribune* newspaper (edited by the show's Marxist military adviser Raymond Fletcher, an MP later outed as a Soviet spy): 'We've heard the poets speak – and we admire them – and we've had *Journey's End*, and we know about the sacrifice of the people who supported the system. But what about our fathers, who went as their dupes? I know I have been accused by some critics of having an anti-officer bias. But the officers have had their day. They've had their theatre. They've had their poetry. They've had their culture long enough.'[64]

But are *Lovely War* and *Journey's End* really so far apart? The short answer is yes – miles. That said, both cast a glowing ray of sadness over the stalls and both evoked the tragic stoicism of the foot soldiers that slogged on. In giving the donkeys and political curs a good kicking, Littlewood was forced to ignore the British success story of 1918, the year of Sherriff's play, presumably because that would have involved explaining how the generals (ninety-seven of whom died or were killed in action with a further 146 wounded or taken prisoner during 1914-18) managed to lead Britain to victory.[65] The show instantly became 'the truth about the war' and replaced the deeply conventional *Journey's End* as the theatre's big-box office response to the war.

---

63   Victor Spinetti, *Up Front*, p.137
64   Interview in *Tribune* 19 April 1963
65   See Gordon Corrigan, *Mud, Blood and Poppycock*, p.194

Journey's End's ambiguity was its making. My guess is that *Lovely War*'s throat-ramming pacifist message was less of a pull than the sparklingly fresh and ironic way it found of reviving the nostalgia and heartbreak of those beguiling trench songs. Anecdotal evidence suggests that lot of veterans of both wars went along to see it and had a great time. In fact it seems to have upset professional historians far more than the military, which is never adverse to a good tune. Today the show (which has proved exceptionally hard to revive on stage since) is still parked like a tank in front of the First World War. The power of the theatre to project a lasting idea is incredible. The show single-handedly taught Britain to hate Haig and the generals. That view has been cemented in place by the rather weedy film version. As objective history, the show is today about as much use as a Noddy book. All the same, *Lovely War* traded in a molten anger that is impossible not to share when you read about the sickening losses on both sides. The First World War was unmentionably dire. Its survivors are remembered for keeping quiet. You still hear the family phrase – "he never talked about it". The cast of *Lovely War* broke the silence. That was its great breakthrough. When the Unknown Warrior – the only body to return to Britain – was buried in Westminster Abbey, they interred him in a ton of imported French soil. *Journey's End* is made of the the same reverential mud. Of course Joan Littlewood hated the play. It was theatrically old-fashioned and, worse still, written by a man who loved king and country. His play didn't blame anyone except (I suspect) himself for having survived.

When you boil it down *Oh What A Lovely War* said 'never again'; *Journey's End*, 'we stuck it'. The gulf between the two plays – one burningly indignant, the other quietly proud – is completely unbridgeable. Yet they are connected in their documentary flavour, their element of nostalgia for the front and their massive success. *Lovely War* came close to beating *Journey's End*'s run at box office in the West End and on Broadway and it gave a generation a war-theme play it could relate to – at least until the Vietnam-era musical *Hair* burst on the scene a few years later. If Sherriff ever saw *Lovely War*, he never mentioned it. But even he was affected by the new mood. In his semi-autobiographical essay in *Promise of Greatness* in 1968, he writes with flashes of uncharacteristic bitterness about the conduct of the war. But by then no one cared what he thought as his war play had become a fossil.

Missing Presumed Dull

I haven't tried in this book to tell the story of Sherriff's writing career after *Journey's End*. But he very nearly gave up the theatre. Sherriff was convinced after the flop of his next play, *Badger's Green*, that his great hit was a fluke. He would become a schoolmaster and that required him to get a degree. He eventually got an offer, aged thirty-four, to study at New College, Oxford where H. A. L. Fisher was Warden.

Sherriff took his mother with him and they rather sweetly rented a house together and she cooked and shopped while he studied and rowed. He found the swotting difficult. He was offered a chance to go to Hollywood and took it, James Whale having invited him over to write the screenplay for *The Invisible Man*, produced by Universal. Sherriff returned to Oxford briefly but he left without a degree for a life of writing. He adapted Galsworthy's *Over the River* (1934) with Colin Clive and A. E. W. Mason's *The Four Feathers* for Alexander Korda. Charles Laughton introduced Sherriff to the book *Goodbye, Mr Chips* by James Hilton but Laughton lost the part to Robert Donat who won an Oscar for it. It was the most Sherriff-like of his screenplays, a sentimental tale set in a private school. Its great weepie moment is when Chips, during the First World War, announces the roll call of the dead in the school chapel, which includes a former pupil (John Mills) and also the German master (Paul Henreid), killed fighting with the Saxon Regiment. It's a magical film, as absorbing as it is sentimental and it even came with a civilised message that not all Germans were 'stinkers' at a time when Britain was bracing itself for another war.

These films gave Sherriff the confidence to return to the stage with a play about St Helena, about Napoleon in captivity, panned by critics. It put Sherriff off stage-writing for twelve more years. The most significant of his later dramas was *Miss Mabel* (it starred Lillian Gish in America) in 1948 and *Home at Seven* (1950), a mystery play (a man 'loses' twenty-four hours of his life) and a touring vehicle for Ralph Richardson.

Sherriff vanished from view. In his autobiography he made a mild complaint about being swept away by the Angry Young Men of the Fifties (a common moan among his generation of writers) but his neglect seemed to have caused him no great anguish. He always lived slightly in the past and was happiest when below the radar. Sherriff's two 1955 films *The Night My Number Came Up* and *The Dam Busters* were his last.

Post-Second World War *Journey's End* became neglected. It is a myth that the play was constantly revived. There was a modest West End production at the Westminster Theatre in 1950, poorly received by critics although endorsed by Montgomery of Alamein in the letters page of *The Times*. But in 1972 a new version reclaimed the play. It was staged by 69 Theatre Company and was directed by Eric Thompson, Emma Thompson's father, at the Mermaid in London before moving to the Cambridge Theatre. It was a big hit. As Stanhope, Peter Egan won Best Actor for the London Theatre Critics Awards and, just as Olivier had, he wore Sherriff's tunic. None of the cast met Sherriff for a discussion about the play. The late James Maxwell played Osborne. He was by all accounts superb as the natural peacemaker who finds himself at war. The show had the future film director Bruce Robinson as Hibbert (*Journey's End* is alluded to at the end of his film *Withnail and I*) and Harry Landis as Mason.

It was reviewed with renewed admiration, most critics respectfully treating the play as a still serviceable, well-constructed piece of sturdy furniture. In *The New Statesman* Benedict Nightingale clobbered the idea that the play was an exposé of the war and that to depict it as such 'was to do so without the consent of the author.'[66] It was the first time

---

66 *The New Statesman*, 26 May 1972

anyone had challenged the critical consensus that it was anti-war. 'Sherriff constructed *Journey's End* out of letters he had written from the front...you feel you are hearing a man who has it all branded into his heart,' wrote Nightingale. The one celebrity dissenter in the audience was Kenneth Williams who wrote in his diary that it was 'reppy, uninspired pedestrian muck'[67] and that the director would be best advised 'to stick it up his arse.'

The general view however, was, that it was a memorial of a play not so much revived as revisited. It went on gathering lichen for another thirty years. There was, however, an enjoyable film version directed by Jack Gold in 1976. The airborne version of *Journey's End*, in which Gielgud played the Headmaster who exhorted the boys 'to play up and play the game.' (I was a £3 a day schoolboy extra on the film and its star Malcolm McDowell – playing the Stanhope part – signed my football shirt!) Its scriptwriter Howard Barker followed the plot of the play quite closely but the film has the long-haired feel of the mid-Seventies – it strafes the Establishment, skewers the juvenility of the officer's mess, introduces a note of lechery and exposes the top brass for not allowing the pilots parachutes on the grounds they would undermine fighting spirit.

The play had had just the occasional London outing since 1972. It opened at the Whitehall Theatre in 1988 with the twenty-five-year-old Jason Connery (son of Sean) making his West End debut as Stanhope and with Nicky Henson as Osborne. The show was a commercial venture and it caught some of the glamour of the original. The dugout collapsed in a coup at the end. The production was conceived as a period piece and was very much a star vehicle for Jason Connery then at the height of his fame as a hugely popular Robin Hood on TV.

Then, in 1998, there was a much sharper, small-scale revival at the King's Head Theatre in London, directed by David Evans Rees, in which Sam West caught the spirit of Stanhope with a very thin moustache and equally clipped tones. Miles

67   Kenneth Williams, *My Diaries*, p.202

Richardson played Osborne. It was impeccably acted and admiringly reviewed, but the show – which bizarrely cut the famous pre-raid recitation of Lewis Carroll – left room for a more expansive look at what Sherriff had actually written. But essentially *Journey's End* got its new lease of life only recently – and that through an upswing of interest in the Great War created by the internet. This is partly thanks to family ancestry websites and easy online access to war records and graves (the Commonwealth War Graves Commission has its own search engine) which make tracking down relatives who fought much easier. Tours of the battlefields and cemeteries of the Western Front are now hugely popular.

The Great War was very much in the ether when *Journey's End* opened in 2004. It came at just the right time, as hits tend to do. It was such a success that in London its longevity echoed the original show; a provisional eight-week run became eighteen months in the West End with several changes of cast. The same production was most recently revived in 2011 for a long national tour and a further return to the West End. It was directed by David Grindley, who had been an assistant at the Chichester Festival Theatre where he worked alongside fifteen different directors, taking over the running of Minerva studio theatre in the wake of Sam Mendes. His big hit as a director was Joe Orton's *Loot* (it transferred to the West End) that in turn led in 2002 to the hit revival of Mike Leigh's famous *Abigail's Party*, which Grindley directed. His *Journey's End* came out of a notion that the producer Phil Cameron had to stage it in tandem with *Another Country*, Julian Mitchell's 1981 play based partly on the Eton schooldays of the Soviet spy Guy Burgess. The idea was to restage both plays as part of a 'Lost Generation' season, which, had it come off, would have been an interesting idea, as the public school system that had provided leadership in the trenches had become by the late Twenties a cradle of treachery. In a short twelve-minute conversation (dictated by a West End parking meter) Grindley convinced his producer he could do the definitive production (a boast he immediately regretted) and was taken on. He used the same team on *Journey's End* as he had on *Abigail's Party*: namely, Jonathan Fensom (design), Jason Taylor (lighting), Gregory Clarke (sound) and Majella Hurley (dialect coach). That quintet would later be reunited in 2012 on another show – Jonathan Lewis's *Our Boys*, a modern army play set on a Woolwich hospital ward full of wounded soldiers.

Grindley, the son of an engineer, has no close family connection with soldiering. But his connection with *Journey's End* was a very personal one all the same. He was introduced to it by his younger brother Michael (who died at the age of nineteen) who had loved the play at school. One of the reasons Grindley's version worked so well was his determination to put himself and the cast entirely at Sherriff's service and not the other way round. His goal was to get to the heart of the thing based on the belief that the play was about a lived experience. He aimed to get the show to open on the exact 75th anniversary of the show's first night in 21 January 1929. Grindley insisted they had to make a feature of that anniversary and also that he had to have control over the casting of Stanhope and Raleigh. 'Ordinarily you would have stars in these parts. But I wanted those two boys to be believably 18 and 21.' He auditioned virtually an entire generation of promising young male talent. 'I couldn't choose between the top two candidates for Stanhope – Geoffrey Streatfeild and Benedict Cumberbatch. Both had been at Manchester University, Geoff had directed Ben in something there so they were very aware of each other. Even though it was a period piece I wanted to make this world in the trenches have an emotional honesty and that would be contemporary and true to the experience. Anyway in the end Geoff got the role after I made him do the revolver scene with Hibbert. He was just tremendous.'

It may have helped a tiny bit that Streatfeild really knew about the army. His brother, Major Richard Streatfeild, is a professional soldier who commanded A Company 4 Rifles with Battlegroup North in Helmand. From there he dictated a series of moving dispatches in his 'Afghan Front Line Diary' for the *Today* programme. A keen blogger, this is what he wrote about his job: 'My personal leadership maxim is a Marxian one: from each according to his ability; to each according to his need. I try to treat everyone equally by treating them all differently. What I know for sure is that if ever things are a little difficult, and there have been a few of those days, I look no further than Riflemen. Common sense, a bit of humour and to be trusted by them to make the right decision despite the associated risks has inspired me.' Except for the reference to Marx, any serving officer at the Western Front would have instantly recognised his style.

David Haig, a big hitter, was next brought in as Osborne. Haig's connection to the play was very deep. Like Osborne, he was a family man. He had been to Rugby and his father (who left the army to run the Hayward Gallery) and grandfather (he won the DSO in the First World War) were both officers. He is also distantly related on his grandmother's side to Field Marshal Haig. David had written a tender play about Kipling's search for his missing son called *My Boy Jack* in which he played Kipling (later filmed with Daniel Radcliffe as his son). Haig's trademark moustache and demeanour ('a woeful face that sums up the bemused tragedy of 20th century militarism,' wrote Aleks Sierz in *Tribune*) made him a natural fit for Osborne and indeed Kipling. Christian Coulson, making his West End debut, was cast as a very fresh-faced Raleigh, looking more sixteen than eighteen but with some showbiz razzle about him having recently appeared in the film *Harry Potter and the Chamber of Secrets*. Grindley also brought in Phil Cornwell – a brilliant comic actor and impressionist – as Mason the cook. Paul Bradley, a Manchester Royal Exchange veteran and former *EastEnders* star, shed entirely new light on working-class ex-ranker Trotter. Both these latter parts, traditionally associated with gor-blimey light comedy relief, the director was determined to invest with equal depth to the others on stage. Grindley's research took him to sites on the Western Front. 'We felt very strongly it was all based on Sherriff's experience in C Company and I wanted to travel the route his company had taken.' He and the set designer Jonathan Fensom – accompanied by Fensom's father, the show's mascot – found a chalky dugout at Vimy that they used as inspiration. All dugouts you visit in France are either fake or tarted up but the one at Vimy had, they thought, just the right note of gangrenous claustrophobia. Grindley wanted to compress the dugout on stage to an absolute bare minimum. 'That visit to Vimy was vital in making us brave enough to make the acting area very small, with just enough space to get around a table and to interrogate a German and no more.' The footprint for the action on stage was tiny. Like an iceberg, most of the set was out of sight. Latex lining on the floor was covered with gravel and sand. The cast was sprayed with water before they went on so that their trousers looked semi-habitable at best. The uniforms were researched and supplied by Taff Gillingham and Richard Ingram. They had been historical advisers to the BBC 2's reality show *The Trench* and later *War Horse*. The ration meat was impersonated by malt loaf. The whisky bottle was in period but they missed a trick in not making it Haig (the blend owned by the Field Marshal's family distilling firm).

In the rehearsal process Grindley devised an idea that much of the men's behavior in the trench was a way of shielding themselves from the grim reality of the position they were in. 'We decided that each of the characters had at least one displacement activity. For example, Stanhope drinks and works, Osborne listens, Trotter eats, and Mason composes menus. Only Hibbert is unable to take his mind off his fear. In order to keep everything active we decided that at no point does anybody reflect on experience, instead they relive it. What I said to the cast was 'don't play fear, play how vigorously each of you is trying to escape the reality of the dugout.' Each character is desperate to occupy his mind with things other than the war.' This is most easily identified in Osborne's monologue when he recounts a story of a wounded man being retrieved from no-man's-land. 'I decided that Osborne was recounting his own experience and when he's telling the story he's reliving it, seeing each moment of it as he's saying it. I felt that by having clear, image by image pictures of the experience in his own mind, the actor would more successfully plant them in ours? It's fascinating to see how in rehearsals, biographies for various characters emerge. Here in his own words is how the director saw the various main characters in the dugout.

Stanhope: 'He is the poster child for the ruling class. Very much the head boy, a vicar's son, a product of the public school system, though with no great sense of entitlement. He's gone over to the front and existed and managed to run a company but at some point he has this terrifying experience at Vimy Ridge. His displacement is to drink and work – anything to avoid thinking of the cost of the responsibility for these men's lives. His other world is in his top pocket – it's a picture of Madge. The light at the end of the tunnel is that he genuinely believes that the war will finish, he will go into rehab somewhere and he will cross the Channel and be the same person he was when he left. The reason he is so obsessed with the arrival of Raleigh is that his arrival totally compromises that possibility.'

Raleigh: 'He's perhaps the most difficult part to play. He doesn't have a displacement activity but he does have a desperate need to reconnect with his childhood. He expects his school holiday relationship with Stanhope to be replicated and it can't be. He comes in with a *Boy's Own* view of the war and the journey for him is an understanding of what the war is. The most difficult scene for Raleigh is that first scene. By the time you get to "the Germans really are decent" you hear Raleigh has got his own voice – that's when it gets a little easier for the actor playing him. He represents the received view of the war, the success of the propaganda. After that raid he is utterly changed – in our version he comes back covered in viscera – and for him the war is not a game any more. With Raleigh the play is a rite of passage. He arrives a boy and he dies a man. Raleigh is presumably like Stanhope was when he first arrived at the front.'

Osborne: 'He is all about listening. For him it's about forgetting himself by absorbing himself in others. As an actor it's very hard because it appears passive but in fact it is very active listening, as it were. He gets people to unlock so that he can be consumed by their problems and not his own. We imagined he went to somewhere like Seaford College [not far from Stane Street mentioned in the play] where he was a beloved schoolmaster. It felt to us as if he was someone who had witnessed the roll call of the dead old boys he had taught and felt he had to join them.

As the play ran longer and longer Osborne was recast. When Philip Franks took over, he brought to the part the schoolmaster side of the character. Philip is a brilliant teacher of the sort you'd wish you had at school. Then we had Malcolm Sinclair – who was superbly a man of the period. Then in Michael Siberry you could believe Osborne was a very tough rugby player.'

Trotter: 'How the actors playing Trotter and Mason the servant interpreted those characters were crucial to the success of the show. I felt very aware that the perception was that this was a middle-class drama. But I felt strongly that Trotter was not there just to make us laugh. The British army was very efficient and quick to judge those who were not up to running the show. Sure, many officers were killed. But a lot of the ones who were not good enough were redeployed. It was a meritocracy. Trotter was there because he was bloody good. He deliberately makes himself the butt of jokes to keep spirits up. But he is a consummate, instinctive soldier and Stanhope knows and loves that. But he doesn't have the relationship with Trotter that he does with Osborne. Trotter has three words which every actor finds a hurdle. When Stanhope accuses him of being unimaginative and always being the same, Trotter says: "little you know." Behind those words is his untold story.'

Mason: 'He thinks about menus. He is trying his best. On the night of Osborne's death he attempts the best thing he has ever done with a jam pudding. For us, the accusation leveled at the play – that it's patronizing and class-ist and that Trotter and Mason are there to be laughed at is, I think, a travesty. Mason and Trotter are central to the team.'

Hibbert: 'Stanhope thinks he will crumble when he puts the gun to his head and threatens to shoot him. In the second half of that scene we see Hibbert through Stanhope's eyes with a new-found respect. That evaporates when he desperately tries to be one of the boys and fails. Hibbert's behaviour is that of a citizen who hasn't made the leap into being a soldier. It's not an anti-war play in that sense. They all know they've got to be there. They understand that the war has got to be fought and they've got to hold the line. Hibbert is simply the one man who can't handle the job.'

When the reviews appeared after the Comedy Theatre first night they were glowing. Geoffrey Streatfeild especially came in for many hurrahs. He managed to retrieve the part from its matinee idol glamour and gave Stanhope a hint of what he might have been like when he first arrived at the front. Charles Spencer in the *Daily Telegraph* complimented the 'portrayal of shredded nerves, alcoholic self-loathing, and the sheer grit and ruthlessness that make him such a magnificent commander.' David Haig was likewise raved for his humane portrayal of the stalwart officer. In the *Jewish Chronicle*, John Nathan was conscious of a party of schoolchildren in the seats near him 'for whom the war must be as distant as the Battle of Culloden Moor – were clearly moved and utterly absorbed.' *Journey's End* had the immediate force of a really good war poem. But while the play rapidly turned into a huge hit, the play still eluded consensus on what it was saying. Talking to Grindley about this, he summed up its spirit: 'It eulogises community. It says, "we are on this raft of an island together." The genius of the thing is its togetherness, which is why the notion of class and snobbery in the play really offends me. It's about us against the world. It's a very British thing. We are staying here. It's do or die.'

Critics saw what they wanted to see; and some wanted to see the First World War in the dock, facing fresh charges of gross futility. Nicholas de Jongh in the *Evening Standard* talked of 'Sherriff's accusatory, politically pointed perspective' – a remark that would have astonished the play's author. Matt Wolf in *International Herald Tribune* declared that, 'Sherriff's specific view of the Great War is that it made no sense.' Toby

Young in the *Spectator* used his column to remind us the war was 'transparently pointless' and 'an utterly worthless cause' and therefore Sherriff was obviously against it – a misrepresentation of the war, the play and the author in one review! My own review in the *Daily Express* was a big thumbs-up but I suggested the play worked despite itself, which is nonsense. It works because it works. Paul Taylor in *The Independent* was the only critic to cite Bernard Shaw's views on Sherriff's typescript in 1928 and to point out the play's crossed wires. 'What makes the play emotionally wrenching, though, is its divided response to romance…the play manages to be keenly insightful about the awful pressures of being hero worshipped, while itself hero-worshipping Stanhope.' Robert Butler (*Independent on Sunday*) who spotted the key thing that Stanhope reveals is 'heroes are heroes because they overcome their own fears.' How Sherriff wished he had had that ability. Michael Coveney (*Daily Mail*) thought the 'play about chaps for chaps is actually a fantastic memoir of the dignity, and futility, of these officers conducting a process far removed from politics and ideology.' In other words, it was a play about how and not why the war was fought. A long view – and equally hard to argue with – was given by Michael Billington in the *Guardian*: 'it wasn't overtly anti-war but that the final ghostly image of the entire company standing in front of the cenotaph, leaves one feeling overwhelmed by the wasteful horror of war.'

War for Britain never stops. The production opened less than a year after 46,000 British troops were sent to Iraq. This was not mentioned in any of the first batch of notices except by Alastair Macaulay in the *Financial Times*: 'I hadn't expected to find it so undated, mainly these men talk much as men might talk today, and I watched wondering how closely the conditions described in this play resembled those experienced by my army nephew in Iraq last year.' A couple of years later, the Iraq war would spectacularly invade the theatre in the award-winning play *Black Watch*, devised by Gregory Burke who walked into a Scottish pub, got the squaddies talking and wrote down what he heard.

It remains easily the best modern play about the British army and the front line.

Grindley's was faithful to the *Journey's End* script, but the key difference from the original 1929 production was his ending. The stage direction requires the dugout to collapse in a shell blast. Grindley and his team didn't do that. Too expensive. So they devised an ending with Stanhope going out as the barrage builds, the light falling on Raleigh's body in the dugout, followed by a blackout in which we get thirty seconds of machine guns and deafening surround-sound shellfire. That then turned into the sound of birdsong followed by the 'Last Post'. The cloth then lifted to reveal the actors frozen like a muster of ghosts, unbowing in front of a stone panel of over 7,000 names (including East Surrey men with characters from the play inserted) from the 54,000 on the Menin Gate memorial to the missing in Ypres. The memorial is at the start of the Menin Road down which endless singing columns of British troops marched into the horrible gloom of the Ypres Salient, that muddy expanse in which so many lives evaporated. The memorial was unveiled in 1927 with the words, 'He is not missing; he is here.' As Grindley put it, 'the idea of having the memorial on stage was to say "you've got to know eleven men here tonight but they are representative of all these others behind them." It's the right ending to the story. It's the end of the journey.'

When J. R. R. Tolkien was a young officer in the trenches, the men in his care were mostly Lancashire weavers, amiable, short and very fond of their rations. He later turned them into Hobbits. Sherriff on the other hand kept his characters fully human, eating, drinking, doing their duty and thinking endlessly of home as they faced danger. It is almost unimaginable that war. We owe Sherriff's generation. Not just the men who fought but also the thousands of courageous families back home whose lives were blighted by grief. *Journey's End*'s lasting qualities are its healing compassion and its sense of remembrance. The anniversary of 2014 would be the ideal date to bring it back.

Plays by R.C. Sherriff
Amateur productions prior to Journey's End

A Hitch in the Proceedings (1921)

The Woods of Meadowside (1923)

Profit and Loss (1923)

Cornlow-in-the-Downs (1924)

Mr Bridie's Finger (1926)

Journey's End (1928), Apollo Theatre: with Laurence Olivier, George Zucco and H. G. Stoker. War play set in the trenches.

Badger's Green (1930), Prince of Wales Theatre: with Felix Aylmer, Louis Goodrich and Horace Hodges. Cricketing comedy about a village under threat from developers.

Windfall (1933), Embassy Theatre: starring Margaret Watson and Hugh E. Wright. Mr Spooner wins a fortune and his friends and family won't let him live his old life.

St Helena (1936), Old Vic Theatre: co-written by Jeanne de Casalis, starring Kenneth Kent. Napoleon's last days in exile.

Miss Mabel (1948), Duchess Theatre: starring Mary Jerrold, Josephine Middleton and Clive Morton. Comedy with murder and a twist.

Home at Seven (1950), Wyndham's Theatre: starring Ralph Richardson and Marion Spencer. An amnesiac bank clerk apparently commits murder during a missing 24 hours of his life.

The White Carnation (1953), Globe Theatre: with Ralph Richardson and Meriel Forbes. A lady librarian becomes the love object of a gentlemanly ghost emanating from a bombsite.

The Long Sunset (1955), Mermaid Theatre: with Joseph O'Connor and Josephine Wilson. Drama set among Romans who stayed behind when the legions left in 410 AD.

The Telescope (1957), Guildford Theatre: with Melvyn Hayes, Edward Woodward and Frank Finlay. Set in London Docklands about a go-ahead vicar, the play was later musicalised by Antony Hopkins as *Johnny The Priest* (1960).

A Shred of Evidence (1960), Duchess Theatre: with Jean Kent and Paul Medway in a melodrama about a man who can't remember if he killed someone on the way home from a rugby club dinner.

Unpublished sources

Sherriff's papers, letters and cuttings (held at Surrey History Centre (SHC) reference 2332 and 3813)

My Diary by R.C. Sherriff (held at Kingston Grammar School)

'The Man From Esher And His Theatre Of War' (producer Simon Hollis) BBC Radio 4

Online sources

The Long, Long Trail (www.1914-1918.net)

The 9/East Surrey Battalion war diary at the SHC (www.surreycc.gov.uk)

Reviews of 2004 _Journey's End_ production are quoted from _Theatre Record_

Books consulted

James Agate, _My Theatre Talks_ (Barker, 1933)

J. M. Barrie, _Courage_ (Hodder and Stoughton, 1922)

George Bishop, _My Betters_ (Heinemann, 1957)

Brian Bond, _The Unquiet Western Front_ (Cambridge University Press, 2002)

Rosa Maria Bracco, _Merchants of Hope: British Middlebrow Writers of the First World War: 1919-1939_ (Berg, 1993)

Malcolm Brown, _The Imperial War Museum Book of 1918, Year of Victory_ (Sidgwick & Jackson, 1998)

Maurice Browne, _Too Late to Lament_ (Gollancz, 1955)

Alan Clark, _The Donkeys_ (Hutchinson, 1961)

George Corrigan, _Mud, Blood and Poppycock_ (Cassell, 2003)

Noël Coward, _Autobiography_ (Methuen, 1986)

James Curtis, _James Whale_ (Scarecrow Press, 1982)

Paul Fussell, _The Great War and Modern Memory_ (Oxford University Press, 1975)

Howard Goorney, _The Theatre Workshop Story_ (Methuen, 1981)

Max Hastings, _Bomber Command_ (Michael Joseph, 1979)

Samuel Hynes, _A War Imagined: The First World War and English Culture_ (The Bodley Head, 1990)

Dominic Hibberd, *The First World War* (Macmillan, 1990)

Dominic Hibberd, *Harold Monro: Poet of the New Age* (Palgrave, 2001)

Richard Huggett, *Binkie Beaumont: Éminence Grise of the West End Theatre 1933-1973* (Hodder & Stoughton, 1989)

Heinz Kosok, *Theatre of War: The First World War in British and Irish Drama* (Palgrave, 2007)

John Lewis-Stempel, *Six Weeks: The Short and Gallant Life of the British Officer in the First World War* (Orion, 2010)

Michael Lucas, *The Journey's End Battalion: the 9th East Surrey in The Great War* (Pen & Sword, 2012)

William H. Mank, *Hollywood's Maddest Doctors* (Midnight Marquee Press, 1999)

Charles Messenger, *Call-to-Arms: the British Army 1914-18* (Cassell, 2005)

Martin Middlebrook, *The Kaiser's Battle* (Allen Lane, 1978)

John Mills, *Up In The Clouds, Gentlemen Please* (Weidenfeld & Nicholson, 1981)

Sean O'Casey, *Rose and Crown* (Macmillan, 1952)

George A Panichas, *The Promise of Greatness: The War of 1914-1918* (Cassell, 1968)

Pearse & Sloman, *History of the East Surrey Regiment* (Spottiswoode, Ballantyne)

Gary Sheffield, *Forgotten Victory* (Headline, 2001)

R.C. Sherriff, *No Leading Lady* (Gollancz, 1968)

Victor Spinetti & Peter Rankin, *Up Front* (Portico, 2006)

Hilton Tims, *Erich Maria Remarque: The Last Romantic* (Constable, 2003)

Dan Todman , *The Great War* (Hambledon, 2005)

Ion Trewin, *Alan Clark: the biography* (Weidenfeld & Nicolson, 2009)

Richard van Emden and Victor Piuk, *Famous: 1914-1918* (Pen & Sword, 2008)

Denis Winter, *Death's Men: Soldiers of the Great War* (Allen Lane, 1978)

Index of Names

Index of Plays, Books and Films

WWW.OBERONBOOKS.COM

Follow us on www.twitter.com/@oberonbooks
& www.facebook.com/oberonbook